THE PRECONCEPTIONS OF
ECONOMIC SCIENCE

The Quarterly Journal of Economics 13 (1899)

BY

THORSTEIN VEBLEN

British Library Cataloguing-in-Publication Data
A catalogue record for this book is available from the
British Library

Contents

Thorstein Veblen

Thorstein Bunde Veblen was born Torsten Bunde Veblen on 30th July 1857 in Cato, Wisconsin, United States, to Norwegian immigrant parents.

Veblen grew up on his parents farm in Nerstrand, Minnesota. This area and others like it were known as little Norways due to the religious and cultural traditions that had been imported from the old country. Although Norwegian was his first language, the young Veblen learned English from neighbours and at school.

His parents put a lot of emphasis on education and hard work and at age seventeen he was sent to study at Carleton College Academy. It was there that he met John Bates Clark (1847–1938) who went on to become a leader in the new field of neoclassical economics. Upon graduating Veblen conducted graduate work under Charles Sanders Pierce (the founder of the pragmatist school in philosophy) at John Hopkins University. He then moved to Yale in 1884 to take a Ph.D. and completed his dissertation on "Ethical Grounds of a Doctrine of Retribution."

Upon leaving Yale he was unable to find a employment. This was partly due to prejudice against Norwegians, and partly because most universities considered him insufficiently educated in Christianity; most academics at the time held divinity degrees. Due to this, Veblen returned to the family farm – ostensibly to recover from malaria – and spent six years there reading voraciously. However, in 1891 he was accepted to study economics as a graduate student at Cornell University. From here on his academic career took off, obtaining his first professional appointment at the University of Chicago – where in 1900 he was promoted to assistant professor – and from there moving on work at institutions including Stanford University and the University of Missouri.

Veblen drew from the work of 19th century intellectuals such as Charles Darwin and Herbert Spencer to develop a 20th century theory of evolutionary economics. He described economic behaviour as socially determined and saw economic organization as a process of ongoing evolution. In his work *The Theory of the Leisure Class* (1899) he outlined how rich and poor alike, attempt to impress others and seek to gain advantage through what Veblen coined "conspicuous consumption" and the ability to engage in "conspicuous leisure." In *The Theory of Business Enterprise* (1904) he used evolutionary analysis to explain the growth of business combinations and trusts.

In the 21st century his ideas have come back into the spotlight as a valid approach for studying the intricacies of economic systems and his theory that humans do not rationally pursue value and utility is one of the cornerstones of the modern discipline of behavioural economics. Veblen made a lasting contribution to his field and has influenced many scholars that have followed him.

Thorstein Veblen died in California on 3rd August 1929, less than three months before the crash of the U.S. Stock market crash which led to the great depression.

THE PRECONCEPTIONS OF
ECONOMIC SCIENCE

I

In an earlier paper(1*) the view has been expressed that the economics handed down by the great writers of a past generation is substantially a taxonomic science. A view of much the same purport, so far as concerns the point here immediately in question, is presented in an admirably lucid and cogent way by Professor Clark in a recent number of this journal.(2*) There is no wish hereby to burden Professor Clark with a putative sponsorship of any ungraceful or questionable generalisations reached in working outward from this main position, but expression may not be denied the comfort which his unintended authentication of the main position affords. It is true, Professor Clark does not speak of taxonomy, but employs the term "statics" which is this connection, through its use by Professor Clark and by other writers eminent in the science, it is fairly to be questioned whether the term can legitimately be used to characterize the received economic theories. The word is borrowed from the jargon of physics, where it is used to designate the theory of bodies at rest or of forces in equilibrium. But there is much in the received economic theories to which the analogy of bodies at rest or of forces in equilibrium will not apply. It is perhaps not too much to say that those articles of economic theory that do not lend themselves to this analogy make up the major portion of the received doctrines. So, for instance, it seems scarcely to the point to speak of the statics of production, exchange, consumption, circulation. There are, no doubt, appreciable elements in the theory of these several processes that may fairly be characterized as statical features of the theory; but the doctrines handed down are after all, in the main, theories of the process discussed under each head, and the theory of a process does not belong in statics. The epithet "statical" would, for instance, have to be wrenched somewhat ungently to make it apply to Quesnay's classic Tableau Economique or to the great body of Physiocratic speculations that take their rise from it. The like is true for Books II. and III. of Adam Smith's Wealth of Nations, as also for considerable portions generation, for much of Marshall's Principles, and for such a modern discussion as Smart's Studies in Economics, as well as for the fruitful activity of the Austrians and of the later representatives of the Historical School.

But to return from this terminological digression. While economic science in the remoter past of its history has been mainly of a taxonomic character, later writers of all schools show something of a divergence from the taxonomic line and an inclination to make the science a genetic account of the economic life process, sometimes even without an ulterior view to the taxonomic value of the results obtained. The divergence from the ancient canons of theoretical formulation is to be taken as an episode of the movement that is going forward in latter-day science generally; and the progressive change which thus affects the ideals and the objective point of the modern sciences seems in its turn to be an expression of that matter-of-fact habit of mind which the prosy but exacting exigencies of life in a modern industrial community breed in men exposed to their unmitigated impact.

In speaking of this matter-of-fact character of the modern sciences it has been broadly characterized as "evolutionary"; and the evolutionary method and the evolutionary ideals have been placed in antithesis to the taxonomic methods and ideals of pre-evolutionary days. But the characteristic attitude, aims, and ideals which are so designated here are by no means peculiar to the group of sciences that are professedly occupied with a process of development, taking that term in its most widely accepted meaning. The latter-day inorganic sciences are in this respect like the organic. They occupy themselves with "dynamic" relations and sequences. The question which they ask is always, What takes place next, and why? Given a situation wrought out out by the forces under inquiry, what follows as the consequence of the situation so wrought out? or what follows upon the accession of further element of force? Even in so non-evolutionary a science as inorganic chemistry the inquiry consistently runs on a process, an active sequence, and the value of the resulting situation as a point of departure for the next step in an interminable cumulative sequence. The last step in the chemist's experimental inquiry into any substance is, What comes of the substance determined? What will it do? What will it lead to, when it is made the point of departure in further chemical action? There is no ultimate term, and no definite solution except in terms of further action. The theory worked out is always a theory of a genetic succession of phenomena, and the relations determined and elaborated into a body of doctrine are always genetic relations. In modern chemistry no cognisance is taken of the honorific bearing of reactions or molecular formulae. The modern chemist, as contrasted with this ancient congener, knows nothing of the worth, elegance, or cogency of the relations that may subsist between the particles of matter with which he busies himself, for any other than the genetic purpose. The spiritual element and the elements of worth and propensity no longer count. Alchemic symbolism and the hierarchical glamour and virtue that once hedged about the nobler and more potent elements and reagents are almost altogether a departed glory of the science. Even the modest imputation of propensity involved in the construction of a scheme of coercive normality, for the putative guidance of reactions, finds little countenance with the later adepts of chemical science. The science has outlived that phase of its development at which the taxonomic feature was the dominant one.

In the modern sciences, of which chemistry is one, there has been a gradual shifting of the point of view from which the phenomena which the science treats of are apprehended and passed upon; and to the historian of chemical science this shifting of the point of view must be a factor of great weight in the development of chemical knowledge. Something of a like nature is true for economic science; and it is the aim here to present, in outline, some of the successive phases that have passed over the spiritual attitude of the adepts of the science, and to point out the manner in which the transition from one point of view to the next has been made.

As has been suggested in the paper already referred to, the characteristic spiritual attitude or point of view of a given generation or group of economists is shown not so much in their detail work as in their higher syntheses -- the terms of their definite formulations -- the grounds of their final valuation of the facts handled for purpose of theory. This line of recondite inquiry into the spiritual past and antecedents of the science has not often been pursued seriously or with singleness of purpose, perhaps because it is, after all, of but slight consequence to the practical efficiency of the present-day science. Still, not a little substantial work has been done towards this end by such writers as Hasbach, Oncken, Bonar, Cannan, and Marshall. And much that is to the purpose is also due to writers outside of economics, for the aims of economic speculation have never been insulated from the work going forward in other lines of inquiry. As would necessarily be the case, the point of view of the enlightened common sense of their time. The spiritual attitude of a given generation of economists is therefore in good part a special outgrowth of the ideals and preconceptions current in the world about them.

So, for instance, it is quite the conventional thing to say that the speculations of the Physiocrats were dominated and shaped by the preconception of Natural Rights. Account has been taken of the effect of natural-rights preconceptions upon the Physiocratic schemes of policy and economic reform, as well as upon the details of their doctrines.(3*) But little has been said of the significance of these preconceptions for the lower courses of the Physiocrats' theoretical structure. And yet that habit of mind to which the natural-rights view is wholesome and adequate is answerable both for the point of departure and for the objective point of the Physiocratic theories, both for the range of facts to which they turned and for the terms in which they were content to formulate their knowledge of the facts which they handled. The failure of their critics to place themselves at the Physiocratic point of view has led to much destructive criticism of their work; whereas, when seen through Physiocratic eyes, such doctrines as those of the net product and of the barrenness of the artisan class appear to be substantially true.

The speculations of the Physiocrats are commonly accounted the first articulate and comprehensive presentation of economic theory that is in line with later theoretical work. The Physiocratic point of view may, therefore, well be taken as the point of departure in an attempt to trace that shifting of aims and norms of procedure that comes into view in the work of later economists when compared with earlier writers.

Physiocratic economics is a theory of the working-out of the Law of Nature (loi naturelle) in its economic bearing, and this Law of Nature is a very simple matter. Les lois naturelles sont on physiques ou morales.

On entend ici, par loi physique, le cours regie de tout evenement physique de l'ordre naturel, evidemment le plus avatageux au genre humain.

On entend ici, par loi morale, the regle de toute action humaine de l'ordre morale, conforme a l'ordre physique evidemment le plus advantageux au genre humain.

Ces lois forment ensemble ce qu'on appelle la loi naturelle. Tous les hommes et toutes les puissances humaines doivent etre soumis a ces lois souveraines, instituees par l'Etre-Supreme: elles sont immuables et irrefragables, et les meilleures lois possible.(4*)

The settled course of material facts tending beneficently to the highest welfare of the human race, -- this is the final term in the Physiocratic speculations. This is the touchstone of substantiality. Conformity to these "immutable and unerring" laws of nature is the test of economic truth. The laws are immutable and unerring, but that does not mean that they rule the course of events with a blind fatality that admits of no exception and no divergence from the direct line. Human nature may, through infirmity or perversity, willfully break over the beneficent trend of the laws of nature; but to the Physiocrat's sense of the matter the laws are none the less immutable and irrefragable on that account. They are not empirical generalisations on the course of phenomena, like the law of falling bodies or of the angle of reflection; although many of the details of their action are to be determined only by observation and experience, helped out, of course, by interpretation of the facts of observation under the light of reason. So, for instance, Turgot, in his Reflections, empirically works out a doctrine of the reasonable course of development through which wealth is accumulated and reaches the existing state of unequal distribution; so also his doctrines of interest and of money. The immutable natural laws are rather of the nature of canons of conduct governing nature than generalisations of mechanical sequence, although in a general way the phenomena of mechanical sequence are details of the conduct of nature working according to these canons of conduct. The great law of the order of nature is of the character of a propensity working to an end, to the accomplishment of a purpose. The processes of nature working under the quasi-spiritual stress of this immanent propensity may be characterised as nature's habits of life. Not that nature is conscious of its travail, and knows and desires the worthy end of its endeavors; but for all that there is a quasi-spiritual nexus between antecedent and consequent in the scheme of operation in which nature is engaged. Nature is not uneasy about interruptions of its course or occasional deflections from the direct line through an untoward conjunction of mechanical causes, nor does the validity of the great overruling law suffer through such an episode. The introduction of a mere mechanically effective causal factor cannot thwart the course of Nature from reaching the goal to which she animistically tends. Nothing can thwart this telological propensity of nature except counter-activity or divergent activity of a similarly teleological kind. Men can break over the law, and have short-sightly and willfully done so; for men are also agents who guide their actions by an end to be achieved. Human conduct is activity of the same kind -- on the same plane of spiritual reality or competency -- as the course of Nature, and it may therefore traverse the latter. The remedy for this short-sighted traffic of misguided human nature is enlightenment, -- "instruction publique et privee des lois de l'ordre naturel."(5*)

The nature in terms of which all knowledge of phenomena -- for the present purpose economic phenomena -- is to be finally synthesised is, therefore, substantially of a quasi-spiritual or animistic character. The laws of nature are in the last resort teleological; they are of the nature of a propensity. The substantial fact in all the sequences of nature is the end to which the sequence naturally tends, not the brute fact of mechanical compulsion or causally effective forces. Economic theory is accordingly the theory (1) of how the efficient causes of the ordre naturel work in an orderly unfolding sequence, guided by the underlying natural law -- the propensity immanent in nature to establish the highest well-being of mankind, and (2) of the conditions imposed upon human conduct by these natural laws in order to reach the ordained goal of supreme human welfare. The conditions so imposed on human conduct are as definitive as the laws and the order by force of which they are imposed; and the theoretical conclusions reached, when these laws and this order are known, are therefore expressions of absolute economic truth. Such conclusions are an expression of reality, but not necessarily of fact.

Now, the objective end of this propensity that determines the course of nature is human well-being. But economic speculation has to do with the workings of nature only so far as regards the ordre physique. And the laws of nature in the ordre physique, working through mechanical sequence, can only work out the physical well-being of man, not necessarily the spiritual. This propensity to the physical well-being of man is therefore the law of nature to which economic science must bring its generalisations, and this law of physical beneficence is the substantial ground of economic truth. Wanting this, all our speculations are vain; but having its authentication they are definitive. The great, typical function, to which all the other functioning of nature is incidental if not subsidiary, is accordingly that of the alimenation, nutrition of mankind. In so far, and only in so far as the physical processes contribute to human sustenance and fullness of life, can they, therefore, further the great work of nature. Whatever processes contribute to human sustenance by adding to the material available for human assimilation and nutrition, by increasing the substantial disposable for human comfort, therefore count towards the substantial end. All other processes, however serviceable in other than this physiological respect, lack the substance of economic reality. Accordingly, human industry is productive, economically speaking, if it heightens the effectiveness of the natural processes out of which the material of human sustenance emerges; otherwise not. The test of productivity, or economic reality in material facts, is the increase of nutritive material. Whatever employment of time or effort does not afford an increase of such material is unproductive, however profitable it may be to the person employed, and however useful or indispensable it may be to the community. The type of such productive industry is the husbandman's employment, which yields a substantial (nutritive) gain. The artisan's work may be useful to the community and profitable to himself, but its economic effect does not extend beyond an alteration of the form in which the material afforded by nature already lies at hand. It is formally productive only, not really productive. It bears no part in the creative or generative work of nature; and therefore it lacks the character of economic substantiality. It does not enhance nature's output of vital force. The artisan's labors, therefore, yield no net product, whereas the husbandman's labors do.

Whatever constitutes a material increment of this output of vital force is wealth, and nothing else is. The theory of value contained in this position has not to do with value according to men's appraisement of the valuable article. Given items of wealth may have assigned to them certain relative values at which they exchange, and these conventional values may differ more or less widely from the natural or intrinsic value of the goods in question; but all that is beside the substantial point. The point in question is not the degree of predilection shown by certain individuals or bodies of men for certain goods. That is a matter of caprice and convention, and it does not directly touch the substantial ground of the economic life. The question of value is a question of the extent to which the given item of wealth forwards the end of nature's unfolding process. It is valuable, intrinsically and really, in so far as it avails the great work which nature has in hand.

Nature, then, is the final term in the Physiocratic speculations. Nature works by impulse and in an unfolding process, under the stress of a propensity to the accomplishment of a given end. The propensity, taken as the final cause that is operative in any situation, furnishes the basis on which to coordinate all our knowledge of those efficient causes through which Nature works to her ends. For the purpose of economic theory proper, this is the ultimate ground of reality to which our quest of economic truth must penetrate. But back of Nature and her works there is, in the Physiocratic scheme of the universe, the Creator, by whose all-wise and benevolent power the order of nature has been established in all the strength and beauty of its inviolate and immutable perfection. But the Physiocratic conception of the Creator is essentially a deistic one: he stands apart from the course of nature which he has established, and keeps his hands off. In the last resort, of course, "Dieu seul est producteur. Les hommes travaillent, receuillent, economisent, conservent; mais economiser n'est par produire."(6*) But this last resort does not bring the Creator into economic theory as a fact to be counted with in formulating economic laws. He serves a homiletical purpose in the Physiocratic speculations rather than fills an office essential to the theory. He comes within the purview of the theory by way of authentication rather than as a subject of inquiry or a term in the formulation of economic knowledge. The Physiocratic God can scarcely be said to be an economic fact, but it is otherwise with that Nature whose ways and means constitute the subject-matter of the Physiocratic inquiry.

When this natural system of the Physiocratic speculation is looked at from the side of the psychology of the investigators, or from that of the logical premises employed, it is immediately recognised as essentially animistic. It runs consistently on animistic ground; but it is animism of a high grade, -- highly integrated and enlightened, but, after all, retaining very much of that primitive force and naivete which characterise the animistic explanations of phenomena in vogue among the untroubled barbarians. It is not the disjected animism of the vulgar, who see a willful propensity -- often a willful perversity -- in given objects or situations to work towards a given outcome, good or bad. It is not the gambler's haphazard sense of fortuitous necessity or the housewife's belief in lucky days, numbers or phases of the moon. The Physiocrat's animism rests on a broader outlook, and does not proceed by such an immediately impulsive imputation of propensity. The teleological element -- the element of propensity -- is conceived in a large way, unified and harmonised, as a comprehensive order of nature as a whole. But it vindicates its standing as a true animism by never becoming fatalistic and never being confused or confounded with the sequence of cause and effect. It has reached the last stage of integration and definition, beyond which the way lies downward from the high, quasi-spiritual ground of animism to the tamer levels of normality and causal uniformities.

There is already discernible a tone of dispassionate and colorless "tendency" about the Physiocratic animism, such as to suggest a wavering towards the side of normality. This is especially visible in such writers as the half-protestant Turgot. In his discussion of the development of farming, for instance, Turgot speaks almost entirely of human motives and the material conditions under which the growth takes place. There is little metaphysics in it, and that little does not express the law of nature in an adequate form. But, after all has been said, it remains true that the Physiocrat's sense of substantiality is not satisfied until he reaches the animistic ground; and it remains true also that the arguments of their opponents made little impression on the Physiocrats so long as they were directed to other than this animistic ground of their doctrine. This is true in great measure even of Turgot, as witness his controversy with Hume. Whatever criticism is directed against them on other grounds is met with impatience, as being inconsequential, if not disingenuous.

(7*)

To an historian of economic theory the source and the line of derivation whereby this precise form of the order-of-nature preconception reached the Physiocrats are of first-rate importance; but it is scarcely a question to be taken up here, -- in part because it is too large a question to be handled here, in part because it has met with adequate treatment at more competent hands,(8*) and in part because it is somewhat beside the immediate point under discussion. This point is the logical, or perhaps better the psychological, value of the Physiocrats' preconception, as a factor in shaping their point of view and the terms of their definitive formulation of economic knowledge. For this purpose it may be sufficient to point out that the preconception in question belongs to the generation in which the Physiocrats lived, and that it is the guiding norm of all serious thought that found ready assimilation into the common-sense views of that time. It is the characteristic and controlling feature of what may be called the common-sense metaphysics of the eighteenth century, especially so far as concerns the enlightened French community.

It is to be noted as a point bearing more immediately on the question in hand that this imputation of final causes to the course of phenomena expresses a spiritual attitude which has prevailed, one might almost say, always and everywhere, but which reached its finest, most effective development, and found its most finished expression, in the eighteenth-century metaphysics. It is nothing recondite; for it meets us at every turn, as a matter of course, in the vulgar thinking of to-day,- in the pulpit and in the market place,- although it is not so ingenuous, nor does it so unquestionedly hold the primacy in the thinking of any class to-day as it once did. It meets us likewise, with but little change of features, at all past stages of culture, late or early. Indeed, it is the most generic feature of human thinking, so far as regards a theoretical or speculative formulation of knowledge. Accordingly, it seems scarcely necessary to trace the lineage of this characteristic preconception of the era of enlightenment, through specific channels, back to the ancient philosophers or jurists of the empire. Some of the specific forms of its expression - as, for instance, the doctrine of Natural Rights - are no doubt traceable through medieval channels to the teachings of the ancients; but there is no need of going over the brook for water, and tracing back to specific teachings the main features of that habit of mind or spiritual attitude of which the doctrines of Natural Rights and the Order of Nature are specific elaborations only. This dominant habit of mind came to the generation of the Physiocrats on the broad ground of group inheritance, not by lineal devolution from any one of the great thinkers of past ages who had thrown its deliverances into a similarly competent form for the use of his own generation.

In leaving the Physiocratic discipline and the immediate sphere of Physiocratic influence for British ground, we are met by the figure of Hume. Here, also, it will be impracticable to go into details as to the remoter line of derivation of the specific point of view that we come upon on making the transition, for reasons similar to those already given as excuse for passing over the similar question with regard to the Physiocratic point of view. Hume is, of course, not primarily an economist; but that placid unbeliever is none the less a large item in any inventory of eighteenth-century economic thought. Hume was not gifted with a facile acceptance of the group inheritance that made the habit of mind of his generation. Indeed, he was gifted with an alert, though somewhat histrionic, skepticism touching everything that was well received. It is his office to prove all things, though not necessarily to hold fast that which is good.

Aside from the strain of affectation discernible in Hume's skepticism, he may be taken as an accentuated expression of that characteristic bent which distinguishes British thinking in his time from the thinking of the Continent, and more particularly of the French. There is in Hume, and in the British community, an insistence on the prosy, not to say the seamy, side of human affairs. He is not content with formulating his knowledge of things in terms of what ought to be or in terms of the objective point of the course of things. He is not even content with adding to the teleological account of phenomena a chain of empirical, narrative generalisations as to the usual course of things. He insists, in season and out of season, on an exhibition of the efficient causes engaged in any sequence of phenomena; and he is skeptical - irreverently skeptical - as to the need or the use of any formulation of knowledge that outruns the reach of his own matter-of-fact, step-by-step argument from cause to effect.

In short, he is too modern to be wholly intelligible to those of his contemporaries who are most neatly abreast of their time. He out-Britishes the British; and, in his footsore quest for a perfectly tame explanation of things, he finds little comfort, and indeed scant courtesy, at the hands of his own generation. He is not in sufficiently naive accord with the range of preconceptions then in vogue.

But, while Hume may be an accentuated expression of a national characteristic, he is not therefore an untrue expression of this phase of British eighteenth-century thinking. The peculiarity of point of view and of method for which he stands has sometimes been called the critical attitude, sometimes the inductive method, sometimes the materialistic or mechanical, and again, though less aptly, the historical method. Its characteristic is an insistence on matter of fact.

This matter-of-fact animus that meets any historian of economic doctrine on his introduction to British economics is a large, but not the largest. feature of the British scheme of early economic thought. It strikes the attention because it stands in contrast with the relative absence of this feature in the contemporary speculations of the Continent. The most potent, most formative habit of thought concerned in the early development of economic teaching on British ground is best seen in the broader generalisations of Adam Smith, and this more potent factor in Smith is a bent that is substantially identical with that which gives consistency to the speculations of the Physiocrats. In Adam Smith the two are happily combined, not to say blended; but the animistic habit still holds the primacy, with the matter-of-fact as a subsidiary though powerful factor. He is said to have combined deduction with induction. The relatively great prominence given the latter marks the line of divergence of British from French economics, not the line of coincidence; and on this account it may not be out of place to look more narrowly into the circumstances to which the emergence of this relatively greater penchant for a matter-of-fact explanation of things in the British community is due.

To explain the characteristic animus for which Hume stands, on grounds that might appeal to Hume, we should have to inquire into the peculiar circumstances - ultimately material circumstances - that have gone to shape the habitual view of things within the British community, and that so have acted to differentiate the British preconceptions from the French, or from the general range of preconceptions prevalent on the Continent. These peculiar formative circumstances are no doubt to some extent racial peculiarities; but the racial complexion of the British community is not widely different from the French, and especially not widely different from certain other Continental communities which are for the present purpose roughly classed with the French. Race difference can therefore not wholly, nor indeed for the greater part, account for the cultural difference of which this difference in preconceptions is an outcome. Through its cumulative effect on institutions the race difference must be held to have had a considerable effect on the habit of mind of the community. but, if the race difference is in this way taken as the remoter ground of an institutional peculiarity, which in its turn has shaped prevalent habits of thought, then the attention may be directed to the proximate causes, the concrete circumstances, through which this race difference has acted, in conjunction with other ulterior circumstances, to work out the psychological phenomena observed. Race differences, it may be remarked, do not so nearly coincide with national lines of demarcation as differences in the point of view from which things are habitually apprehended or differences in the standards according to which facts are rated.

If the element of race difference be not allowed definitive weight in discussing national peculiarities that underlie the deliverances of common sense, neither can these national peculiarities be confidently traced to a national difference in the transmitted learning that enters into the common-sense view of things. So far as concerns the concrete facts embodied in the learning of the various nations within the European culture, these nations make up but a single community. What divergence is visible does not touch the character of the positive information with which the learning of the various nations is occupied. Divergence is visible in the higher syntheses, the methods of handling the material of knowledge, the basis of valuation of the facts taken up, rather than in the material of knowledge. But this divergence must be set down to a cultural difference, a difference of point of view, not to a difference in inherited information. When a given body of information passes the national frontiers it acquires a new complexion, a new national, cultural physiognomy. It is this cultural physiognomy of learning that is here under inquiry, and a comparison of early French economics (the Physiocrats) with early British economics (Adam Smith) is here entered upon merely with a view to making out what significance this cultural physiognomy of the science has for the past progress of economic speculation.

The broad features of economic speculation. as it stood at the period under consideration, may be briefly summed up, disregarding the element of policy, or expediency, which is common to both groups of economists, and attending to their theoretical work alone. With the Physiocrats, as with Adam Smith, there are two main points of view from which economic phenomena are treated: (a) the matter-of-fact point of view or preconception, which yields a discussion of causal sequences and correlations; and (b) what, for want of a more expressive word, is here called the animistic point of view or preconception, which yields a discussion of teleological sequences and correlations, a discussion of the function of this and that "organ," of the legitimacy of this or the other range of facts. The former preconception is allowed a larger scope in the British than in the French economics: there is more of "induction" in the British. The latter preconception is present in both, and is the definitive element in both but the animistic element is more colorless in the British, it is less constantly in evidence, and less able to stand alone without the support of arguments from cause to effect. Still, the animistic element is the controlling factor in the higher syntheses of both; and for both alike it affords the definitive ground on which the argument finally comes to rest. In neither group of thinkers is the sense of substantiality appeased until this quasi-spiritual ground. given by the natural propensity of the course of events, is reached. But the propensity in events, the natural or normal course of things, as appealed to by the British speculators, suggests less of an imputation of willpower, or personal force, to the propensity in question. It may be added, as has already been said in another place, that the tacit imputation of will-power or spiritual consistency to the natural or normal course of events has progressively weakened in the later course of economic speculation, so that in this respect, the British economists of the eighteenth century may be said to represent a later phase of economic inquiry than the Physiocrats.

Unfortunately, but unavoidably, if this question as to the cultural shifting of the point of view in economic science is taken up from the side of the causes to which the shifting is traceable, it will take the discussion back to ground on which an economist must at best feel himself to be but a raw layman, with all a layman's limitations and ineptitude, and with the certainty of doing badly what might be done well by more competent hands. But, with a reliance on charity where charity is most needed, it is necessary to recite summarily what seems to be the psychological bearing of certain cultural facts.

A cursory acquaintance with any of the more archaic phases of human culture enforces the recognition of this fact,- that the habit of construing the phenomena of the inanimate world in animistic terms prevails pretty much universally on these lower levels. Inanimate phenomena are apprehended to work out a propensity to an end; the movements of the elements are construed in terms of quasi-personal force. So much is well authenticated by the observations on which anthropologists and ethnologists draw for their materials. This animistic habit. it may be said, seems to be more effectual and far-reaching among those primitive communities that lead a predatory life.

But along with this feature of archaic methods of thought or of knowledge, the picturesqueness of which has drawn the attention of all observers, there goes a second feature, no less important for the purpose in hand, though less obtrusive. The latter is of less interest to the men who have to do with the theory of cultural development, because it is a matter of course. This second feature of archaic thought is the habit of also apprehending facts in non-animistic, or impersonal, terms. The imputation of propensity in no case extends to all the mechanical facts in the case. There is always a substratum of matter of fact, which is the outcome of an habitual imputation of causal sequence, or, perhaps better, an imputation of mechanical continuity, if a new term be permitted. The agent, thing, fact, event. or phenomenon, to which propensity, will-power, or purpose, is imputed, is always apprehended to act in an environment which is accepted as spiritually inert. There are always opaque facts as well as self-directing agents. Any agent acts through means which lend themselves to his use on other grounds than that of spiritual compulsion, although spiritual compulsion may be a large feature in any given case.

The same features of human thinking, the same two complementary methods of correlating facts and handling them for the purposes of knowledge, are similarly in constant evidence in the daily life of men in our own community. The question is, in great part, which of the two bears the greater part in shaping human knowledge at any given time and within any given range of knowledge or of facts.

Other features of the growth of knowledge, which are remoter from the point under inquiry, may be of no less consequence to a comprehensive theory of the development of culture and of thought; but it is of course out of the question here to go farther afield. The present inquiry will have enough to do with these two. No other features are correlative with these, and these merit discussion on account of their intimate bearing on the point of view of economics. The point of interest with respect to these two correlative and complementary habits of thought is the question of how they have fared under the changing exigencies of human culture; in what manner they come, under given cultural circumstances, to share the field of knowledge between them; what is the relative part of each in the composite point of view in which the two habits of thought express themselves at any given cultural stage.

The animistic preconception enforces the apprehension of phenomena in terms generically identical with the terms of personality or individuality. As a certain modern group of psychologists would say, it imputes to objects and sequences an element of habit and attention similar in kind, though not necessarily in degree, to the like spiritual attitude present in the activities of a personal agent. The matter-of-fact preconception, on the other hand, enforces a handling of facts without imputation of personal force or attention, but with an imputation of mechanical continuity, substantially the preconception which has reached a formulation at the hands of scientists under the name of conservation of energy or persistence of quantity. Some appreciable resort to the latter method of knowledge is unavoidable at any cultural stage, for it is indispensable to all industrial efficiency. All technological processes and all mechanical contrivances rest, psychologically speaking, on this ground. This habit of thought is a selectively necessary consequence of industrial life, and, indeed, of all human experience in making use of the material means of life. It should therefore follow that, in a general way, the higher the culture, the greater the share of the mechanical preconception in shaping human thought and knowledge, since, in a general way, the stage of culture attained depends on the efficiency of industry. The rule, while it does not hold with anything like extreme generality, must be admitted to hold to a good extent; and to that extent it should hold also that, by a selective adaptation of men's habits of thought to the exigencies of those cultural phases that have actually supervened, the mechanical method of knowledge should have gained in scope and range. Something of the sort is borne out by observation.

A further consideration enforces the like view. As the community increases in size, the range of observation of the individuals in the community also increases; and continually wider and more far-reaching sequences of a mechanical kind have to be taken account of. Men have to adapt their own motives to industrial processes that are not safely to be construed in terms of propensity, predilection, or passion. Life in an advanced industrial community does not tolerate a neglect of mechanical fact; for the mechanical sequences through which men, at an appreciable degree of culture, work out their livelihood, are no respecters of persons or of will-power. Still, on all but the higher industrial stages, the coercive discipline of industrial life, and of the scheme of life that inculcates regard for the mechanical facts of industry, is greatly mitigated by the largely haphazard character of industry, and by the great extent to which man continues to be the prime mover in industry. So long as industrial efficiency is chiefly a matter of the handicraftsman's skill, dexterity, and diligence, the attention of men in looking to the industrial process is met by the figure of the workman, as the chief and characteristic factor; and thereby it comes to run on the personal element in industry.

But, with or without mitigation, the scheme of life which men perforce adopt under exigencies of an advanced industrial situation shapes their habits of thought on the side of their behavior, and thereby shapes their habits of thought to some extent for all purposes. Each individual is but a single complex of habits of thought, and the same psychical mechanism that expresses itself in one direction as conduct expresses itself in another direction as knowledge. The habits of thought formed in the one connection, in response to stimuli that call for a response in terms of conduct, must, therefore, have their effect when the same individual comes to respond to stimuli that call for a response in terms of knowledge. The scheme of thought or of knowledge is in good part a reverberation of the scheme of life. So that, after all has been said, it remains true that with the growth of industrial organization and efficiency there must, by selection and by adaptation, supervene a greater resort to the mechanical or dispassionate method of apprehending facts.

But the industrial side of life is not the whole of it, nor does the scheme of life in vogue in any community or at any cultural stage comprise industrial conduct alone. The social, civic, military, and religious interests come in for their share of attention, and between them they commonly take up by far the larger share of it. Especially is this true so far as concerns those classes among whom we commonly look for a cultivation of knowledge for knowledge's sake. The discipline which these several interests exert does not commonly coincide with the training given by industry. So the religious interest, with its canons of truth and of right living, runs exclusively on personal relations and the adaptation of conduct to the predilections of a superior personal agent. The weight of its discipline, therefore, falls wholly on the animistic side. It acts to heighten our appreciation of the spiritual bearing of phenomena and to discountenance a matter-of-fact apprehension of things. The skeptic of the type of Hume has never been in good repute with those who stand closest to the accepted religious truths. The bearing of this side of our culture upon the development of economics is shown by what the mediaeval scholars had to say on economic topics.

The disciplinary effects of other phases of life, outside of the industrial and the religious, is not so simple a matter; but the discussion here approaches nearer to the point of immediate inquiry, -- namely, the cultural situation in the eighteenth century, and its relation to economic speculation, -- and this ground of interest in the question may help to relieve the topic of the tedium that of right belongs to it.

In the remoter past of which we have records, and even in the more recent past, Occidental man, as well as man elsewhere, has eminently been a respecter of persons. Wherever the warlike activity has been a large feature of the community's life, much of human conduct in society has proceeded on a regard for personal force. The scheme of life has been a scheme of personal aggression and subservience, partly in the naive form, partly conventionalised in a system of status. The discipline of social life for the present purpose, in so far as its canons of conduct rest on this element of personal force in the unconventionalised form, plainly tends to the formation of a habit of apprehending and coordinating facts from the animistic point of view. So far as we have to do with life under a system of status, the like remains true, but with a difference. The regime of status inculcates an unremitting and very nice discrimination and observance of distinctions of personal superiority and inferiority. To the criterion of personal force, or will-power, taken in its immediate bearing on conduct, is added the criterion of personal excellence-in-general, regardless of the first-hand potency of the given person as an agent. This criterion of conduct requires a constant and painstaking imputation of personal value, regardless of fact. The discrimination enjoined by the canons of status proceeds on an invidious comparison of persons in respect of worth, value, potency, virtue, which must, for the present purpose, be taken as putative. The greater or less personal value assigned a given individual or a given class under the canons of status is not assigned on the ground of visible efficiency, but on the ground of a dogmatic allegation accepted on the strength of an uncontradicted categorical affirmation simply. The canons of status hold their ground by force of preemption. Where distinctions of status are based on a putative worth transmitted by descent from honorable antecedents, the sequence of transmission to which appeal is taken as the arbiter of honor is of a putative and animistic character rather than a visible mechanical continuity. The habit of accepting as final what is prescriptively right in the affairs of life has as its reflex in the affairs of knowledge the formula, Quid ab omnibus, quid ubique creditur credendum est.

Even this meager account of the scheme of life that characterises a regime of status should serve to indicate what is its disciplinary effect in shaping habits of thought, and therefore in shaping the habitual criteria of knowledge and of reality. A culture whose institutions are a framework of invidious comparisons implies, or rather involves and comprises, a scheme of knowledge whose definitive standards of truth and substantiality are of an animistic character; and, the more undividedly the canons of status and ceremonial honor govern the conduct of the community, the greater the facility with which the sequence of cause and effect is made to yield before the higher claims of a spiritual sequence or guidance in the course of events. Men consistently trained to an unremitting discrimination of honor, worth, and personal force in their daily conduct, and to whom these criteria afford the definitive ground of sufficiency in coOrdinating facts for the Purposes of life, will not be satisfied to fall short of the like definitive ground of sufficiency when they come to coordinate facts for the purposes of knowledge simply. The habits formed in un folding his activity in one direction, under the impulse of a given interest, assert themselves when the individual comes to unfold his activity in any other direction, under the impulse of any other interest. If his last resort and highest criterion of truth in conduct is afforded by the element of personal force and invidious comparison, his sense of substantiality or truth in the quest of knowledge will be satisfied only when a like definitive ground of animistic force and invidious comparison is reached. But when such ground is reached he rests content and pushes the inquiry no farther. In his practical life he has acquired the habit of resting his case on an authentic deliverance as to what is absolutely right. This absolutely right and good final term in conduct has the character of finality only when conduct is construed in a ceremonial sense; that is to say, only when life is conceived as a scheme of conformity to a purpose outside and beyond the process of living. Under the regime of status this ceremonial finality is found in the concept of worth or honor. In the religious domain it is the concept of virtue, sanctity, or tabu. Merit lies in what one is, not in what one does. The habit of appeal to ceremonial finality, formed in the school of status, goes with the individual in his quest of knowledge, as a dependence upon a similarly authentic norm of absolute truth, -- a similar seeking of a final term outside and beyond the range of knowledge.

The discipline of social and civic life under a regime of status, then, reinforces the discipline of the religious life; and the outcome of the resulting habituation is that the canons of knowledge are cast in the animistic mold and converge to a ground of absolute truth, and this absolute truth is of a ceremonial nature. Its subject-matter is a reality regardless of fact. The outcome, for science, of the religious and social life of the civilisation of status, in Occidental culture, was a structure of quasi-spiritual appreciations and explanations, of which astrology, alchemy, and medieval theology and metaphysics are competent, though somewhat one-sided, exponents. Throughout the range of this early learning the ground of correlation of phenomena is in part the supposed relative potency of the facts correlated. but it is also in part a scheme of status, in which facts are scheduled according to a hierarchical gradation of worth or merit, having only a ceremonial relation to the observed phenomena. Some elements (some metals. for instance) are noble, others base; some planets, on grounds of ceremonial efficacy, have a sinister influence, others a beneficent one; and it is a matter of serious consequence whether they are in the ascendant, and so on.

The body of learning through which the discipline of animism and invidious comparison transmitted its effects to the science of economics was what is known as natural theology, natural rights, moral philosophy, and natural law. These several disciplines or bodies of knowledge had wandered far from the naive animistic standpoint at the time when economic science emerged, and much the same is true as regards the time of the emergence of other modern sciences. But the discipline which makes for an animistic formulation of knowledge continued to hold the primacy in modern culture, although its dominion was never altogether undivided or unmitigated. Occidental culture has long been largely an industrial culture; and, as already pointed out, the discipline of industry, and of life in an industrial community, does not favor the animistic preconception. This is especially true as regards industry which makes large use of mechanical contrivances. The difference in these respects between Occidental industry and science, on the one hand, and the industry and science of other cultural regions, on the other hand, is worth noting in this connection. The result has been that the sciences, as that word is understood in later usage, have come forward gradually, and in a certain rough parallelism with the development of industrial processes and industrial organisation. It is possible to hold that both modern industry (of the mechanical sort) and modern science center about the region of the North Sea. It is still more palpably true that within this general area the sciences, in the recent past, show a family likeness to the civil and social institutions of the communities in which they have been cultivated, this being true to the greatest extent of the higher or speculative sciences; that is, in that range of knowledge in which the animistic preconception can chiefly and most effectively find application. There is, for instance, in the eighteenth century a perceptible parallelism between the divergent character of British and Continental culture and institutions, on the one hand, and the dissimilar aims of British and Continental speculation, on the other hand.

Something has already been said of the difference in preconceptions between the French and the British economists of the eighteenth century. It remains to point out the correlative cultural difference between the two communities, to which it is conceived that the difference in scientific animus is in great measure due. It is, of course, only the general features, the general attitude of the speculators, that can be credited to the difference in culture. Differences of detail in the specific doctrines held could be explained only on a much more detailed analysis than can be entered on here, and after taking account of facts which cannot here be even allowed for in detail.

Aside from the greater resort to mechanical contrivances and the larger scale of organisation in British industry, the further cultural peculiarities of the British community run in the same general direction. British religious life and beliefs had less of the element of fealty personal or discretionary mastery and subservience -- and more of a tone of fatalism. The civil institutions of the British had not the same rich personal content as those of the French. The British subject owned allegiance to an impersonal law rather than to the person of a superior. Relatively, it may be said that the sense of status, as a coercive factor, was in abeyance in the British community. Even in the warlike enterprise of the British community a similar characteristic is traceable. Warfare is, of course, a matter of personal assertion. Warlike communities and classes are necessarily given to construing facts in terms of personal force and personal ends. They are always superstitious. They are great sticklers for rank and precedent, and zealously cultivate those distinctions and ceremonial observances in which a system of status expresses itself. But, while warlike enterprise has by no means been absent from the British scheme of life, the geographical and strategic isolation of the British community has given a characteristic turn to their military relations. In recent times British warlike operations have been conducted abroad. The military class has consequently in great measure been segregated out from the body of the community, and the ideals and prejudices of the class have not been transfused through the general body with the same facility and effect that they might otherwise have had. The British community at home has seen the campaign in great part from the standpoint of the "sinews of war."

The outcome of all these national peculiarities of circumstance and culture has been that a different scheme of life has been current in the British community from what has prevailed on the Continent. There has resulted the formation of a different body of habits of thought and a different animus in their handling of facts. The preconception of causal sequence has been allowed larger scope in the correlation of facts for purposes of knowledge; and, where the animistic preconception has been resorted to, as it always has in the profounder reaches of learning, it has commonly been an animism of a tamer kind.

Taking Adam Smith as an exponent of this British attitude in theoretical knowledge, it is to be noted that, while he formulates his knowledge in terms of a propensity (natural laws) working teleologically to an end, the end or objective point which controls the formulation has not the same rich content of vital human interest or advantage as is met with in the Physiocratic speculations. There is perceptibly less of an imperions tone in Adam Smith's natural laws than in those of the contemporary French economists. It is true, he sums up the institutions with which he deals in terms of the ends which they should subserve, rather than in terms of the exigencies and habits of life out of which they have arisen; but he does not with the same tone of finality appeal to the end subserved as a final cause through whose coercive guidance the complex of phenomena is kept to its appointed task. Under his hands the restraining, compelling agency retires farther into the background, and appeal is taken to it neither so directly nor on so slight provocation.

But Adam Smith is too large a figure to be disposed of in a couple of concluding paragraphs. At the same time his work and the bent which he gave to economic speculation are so intimately bound up with the aims and bias that characterise economics in its next stage of development that he is best dealt with as the point of departure for the Classical School rather than merely as a British counterpart of Physiocracy. Adam Smith will accordingly be considered in immediate connection with the bias of the classical school and the incursion of utilitarianism into economics.

NOTES:

1. "Why is Economics not an Evolutionary Science?" Quarterly Journal of Economics, July, 1898.

2. "The Future of Economic Theory," ibid., October, 1898.

3. See, for instance, Hasbuch, Allgemeine philosophische Grundlagen der von Francois Quesnay und Adam Smith begrundeten

politischen Oekonomie.

4. Quesnay, Droit Naturel, ch. v. (Ed. Daire, Physiocrates, pp. 52-53).

5. Quesnay, Droit Naturel, ch. v. (Ed. Daire, Physiocrates, p. 53).

6. Dupont de Nemours, Correspondence avec J.-B. Say (Ed. Daire, Physiocrates, premiere partie, p. 399).

7. See, for instance, the concluding chapters of La Riviere's Ordre Naturel des Societies Politiques.

8. E.g., Hasbuch, loc. cit.; Bonar, Philosophy and Political Economy, Book II; Ritchie, Natural Rights.

II

ADAM SMITH'S animistic bent asserts itself more plainly and more effectually in the general trend and aim of his discussion than in the details of theory. "Adam Smith's Wealth of Nations is, in fact, so far as it has one single purpose, a vindication of the unconscious law present in the separate actions of men when these actions are directed by a certain strong personal motive."(1*) Both in the Theory of the Moral Sentiments and in the Wealth of Nations there are many passages that testify to his abiding conviction that there is a wholesome trend in the natural course of things, and the characteristically optimistic tone in which he speaks for natural liberty is but an expression of this conviction. An extreme resort to this animistic ground occurs in his plea for freedom of investment.(2*)

In the proposition that men are "led by an invisible hand," Smith does not fall back on a meddling Providence who is to set human affairs straight when they are in danger of going askew. He conceives the Creator to be very continent in the matter of interference with the natural course of things. The Creator has established the natural order to serve the ends of human welfare; and he has very nicely adjusted the efficient causes comprised in the natural order, including human aims and motives, to this work that they are to accomplish. The guidance of interposition, the invisible hand takes place not by way of interposition, but through a comprehensive scheme of contrivances established from the beginning. For the purpose of economic theory, man is conceived to be consistently self-seeking; but this economic man is a part of the mechanism of nature, and his self-seeking traffic is but a means whereby, in the natural course of things, the general welfare is worked out. The scheme as a whole is guided by the end to be reached, but the sequence of events through which the end is reached is a causal sequence which is not broken into episodically. The benevolent work of guidance was performed in first establishing an ingenious mechanism of forces and motives capable of accomplishing an ordained result, and nothing beyond the enduring constraint of an established trend remains to enforce the divine purpose in the resulting natural course of things.

The sequence of events, including human motives and human conduct, is a causal sequence; but it is also something more, or, rather, there is also another element of continuity besides that of brute cause and effect, present even in the step-by-step process whereby the natural course of things reaches its final term. The presence of such a quasi-spiritual or non-causal element is evident from two (alleged) facts. (1) The course of things may be deflected from the direct line of approach to that consummate human welfare which is its legitimate end. The natural trend of things may be overborne by an untoward conjuncture of causes. There is a distinction, often distressingly actual and persistent, between the legitimate and the observed course of things. If "natural," in Adam Smith's use, meant necessary, in the sense of causally determined, no divergence of events from the natural or legitimate course of things would be possible. If the mechanism of nature, including man, were a mechanically competent contrivance for achieving the great artificer's design, there could be no such episodes of blundering and perverse departure from the direct path as Adam Smith finds in nearly all existing arrangements. Institutional facts would then be "natural."(3*) (2) When things have gone wrong, they will right themselves if interference with the natural course ceases; whereas, in the case of a causal sequence simply, the mere cessation of interference will not leave the outcome the same as if no interference had taken place. This recuperative power of nature is of an extra-mechanical character. The continuity of sequence by force of which the natural course of things prevails is, therefore, not of the nature of cause and effect, since it bridges intervals and interruptions in the causal sequence.(4*) Adam Smith's use of the term "real " in statements of theory -- as, for example, "real value," "real price"(5*) -- is evidence to this effect. "Natural" commonly has the same meaning as "real" in this connection.(6*)

Both "natural" and "real" are placed in contrast with the actual; and, in Adam Smith's apprehension, both have a substantiality different from and superior to facts. The view involves a distinction between reality and fact, which survives in a weakened form in the theories of "normal" prices, wages, profits, costs, in Adam Smith's successors.

This animistic prepossession seems to pervade the earlier of his two monumental works in a greater degree than the later. In the Moral Sentiments recourse is had to the teleological ground of the natural order more freely and with perceptibly greater insistence. There seems to be reason for holding that the animistic preconception weakened or, at any rate, fell more into the background as his later work of speculation and investigation proceeded. The change shows itself also in some details of his economic theory, as first set forth in the Lectures, and afterwards more fully developed in the Wealth of Nations. So, for instance, in the earlier presentation of the matter," the division of labor is the immediate cause of opulence"; and this division of labor, which is the chief condition of economic well-being, "flows from a direct propensity in human nature for one man to barter with another."(7*) The "propensity" in question is here appealed to as a natural endowment immediately given to man with a view to the welfare of human society, and without any attempt at further explanation of how man has come by it. No causal explanation of its presence or character is offered. But the corresponding passage of the Wealth of Nations handles the question more cautiously.(8*) Other parallel passages might be compared, with much the same effect. The guiding hand has withdrawn farther from the range of human vision.

However, these and other like filial expressions of a devout optimism need, perhaps, not be taken as integral features of Adam Smith's economic theory, or as seriously affecting the character of his work as an economist. They are the expression of his general philosophical and theological views, and are significant for the present purpose chiefly as evidences of an animistic and optimistic bent. They go to show what is Adam Smith's accepted ground of finality, -- the ground to which all his speculations on human affairs converge; but they do not in any great degree show the teleological bias guiding his formulation of economic theory in detail.

The effective working of the teleological bias is best seen in Smith's more detailed handling of economic phenomena -- in his discussion of what may loosely be called economic institutions -- and in the criteria and principles of procedure by which he is guided in incorporating these features of economic life into the general structure of his theory. A fair instance, though perhaps not the most telling one, is the discussion of the "real and nominal price," and of the "natural and market price" of commodities, already referred to above.(9*) The "real" price of commodities is their value in terms of human life. At this point Smith differs from the Physiocrats, with whom the ultimate terms of value are afforded by human sustenance taken as a product of the functioning of brute nature; the cause of the difference being that the Physiocrats conceived the natural order which works towards the material well-being of man to comprise the nonhuman environment only, whereas Adam Smith includes man in this concept of the natural order, and, indeed, makes him the central figure in the process of production. With the Physiocrats, production is the work of nature: with Adam Smith, it is the work of man and nature, with man in the foreground. In Adam Smith, therefore, labor the final term in valuation. This "real" value of commodities is the value imputed to them by the economist under the stress of his teleological preconception. It has little, if any, place in the course of economic events, and no bearing on human affairs, apart from the sentimental influence which such a preconception in favor of a "real value " in things may exert upon men's notions of what is the good and equitable course to pursue in their transactions. It is impossible to gauge this real value of goods; it cannot be measured or expressed in concrete terms. Still, if labor exchanges for a varying quality of goods, "it is their value which varies, not that of the labor which purchases them."(10*) The values which practically attach to goods in men's handling of them are conceived to be determined without regard to the real value which Adam Smith imputes to the goods; but, for all that, the substantial fact with respect to these market values is their presumed approximation to the real values teleologically imputed to the goods under the guidance of inviolate natural laws. The real, or natural, value of articles has no causal relation to the value at which they exchange. The discussion of how values are determined in practice runs on the motives of the buyers and sellers, and the relative advantage enjoyed by the parties to the transaction.(11*) It is a discussion of a process of valuation, quite unrelated to the "real," or "natural," price of things, and quite unrelated to the grounds on which things are held to come by their real, or natural, price; and yet, when the complex process of valuation has been traced out in terms of human motives and the exigencies of the market, Adam Smith feels that he has only cleared the ground. He then turns to the serious business of accounting for value and price theoretically, and making the ascertained facts articulate with his teleological theory of economic life.(12*)

The occurrence of the words "ordinary" and "average" in this connection need not be taken too seriously. The context makes it plain that the equality which commonly subsists between the ordinary or average rates, and the natural rates, is a matter of coincidence, not of identity. Not only are there temporary deviations, but there may be a permanent divergence between the ordinary and the natural price of a commodity; as in case of a monopoly or of produce grown under peculiar circumstances of soil or climate.(13*)

The natural price coincides with the price fixed by competition, because competition means the unimpeded play of those efficient forces through which the nicely adjusted mechanism of nature works out the design to accomplish which it was contrived. The natural price is reached through the free interplay of the factors of production, and it is itself an outcome of production. Nature, including the human factor, works to turn out the goods; and the natural value of the goods is their appraisement from the standpoint of this productive process of nature. Natural value is a category of production: whereas, notoriously exchange value or market price is a category of distribution. And Adam Smith's theoretical handling of market price aims to show how the factors of human predilection and human wants at work in the higgling of the market bring about a result in passable consonance with the natural laws that are conceived to govern production.

The natural price is a composite result of the blending of the three "component parts of the price of commodities," -- the natural wages of laborer, the natural profits of stock, and the natural rent of land; and each of these three components is in its turn the measure of the productive effect of the factor to which it pertains. The further discussion of these shares in distribution aims to account for the facts of distribution on the ground of the productivity of the factors which are held to share the product between them. That is to say, Adam Smith's preconception of a productive natural process as the basis of his economic theory dominates his aims and procedure, when he comes to deal with phenomena that cannot be stated in terms of production. The causal sequence in the process of distribution is, by Adam Smith's own showing, unrelated to the causal sequence in the process of production; but, since the latter is the substantial fact, as viewed from the standpoint of a teleological natural order, the former must be stated in terms of the latter before Adam Smith's sense of substantiality, or "reality," is satisfied. Something of the same kind is, of course, visible in the Physiocrats and in Cantillon. It amounts to an extension of the natural-rights preconception to economic theory. Adam Smith's discussion of distribution as a function of productivity might be traced in detail through his handling of Wages, Profits, and Rent; but, since the aim here is a brief characterisation only, and not an exposition, no farther pursuit of this point seems feasible.

It may, however, be worth while to point out another line of influence along which the dominance of the teleological preconception shows itself in Adam Smith. This is the normalisation of data, in order to bring them into consonance with an orderly course of approach to the putative natural end of economic life and development. The result of this normalisation of data is, on the one and, the use of what James Steuart calls "conjectural history" in dealing with past phases of economic life, and, on the other hand, a statement of present-day phenomena in terms of what legitimately ought to be according to the God-given end of life rather than in terms of unconstrued observation. Account is taken of the facts (supposed or observed) ostensibly in terms of causal sequence, but the imputed causal sequence is construed to run on lines of teleological legitimacy.

A familiar instance of this "conjectural history," in a highly and effectively normalized form, is the account of "that early and rude state of society which precedes both the accumulation of stock and the appropriation of land." (14*) It is needless at this day to point out that this "early and rude state," in which "the whole produce of labor belongs to the laborer," is altogether a figment. The whole narrative, from the putative origin down, is not only supposititious, but it is merely a schematic presentation of what should have been the course of past development, in order to lead up to that ideal economic situation which would satisfy Adam Smith's preconception.(15*) As the narrative comes nearer the region of known latter-day facts, the normalisation of the data becomes more difficult and receives more detailed attention; but the change in method is a change of degree rather than of kind. In the "early and rude state" the coincidence of the "natural" and the actual course of events is immediate and undisturbed, there being no refractory data at hand; but in the later stages and in the present situation, where refractory facts abound, the coordination is difficult, and the coincidence can be shown only by a free abstraction from phenomena that are irrelevant to the teleological trend and by a laborious interpretation of the rest. The facts of modern life are intricate, and lend themselves to statement in the terms of the theory only after they have been subjected to a "higher criticism."

The chapter "Of the Origin and Use of Money"(16*) is an elegantly normalised account of the origin and nature of an economic institution, and Adam Smith's further discussion of money runs on the same lines. The origin of money is stated in terms of the purpose which money should legitimately serve in such a community as Adam Smith considered right and good, not in terms of the motives and exigencies which have resulted in the use of money and in the gradual rise of the existing method of payment and accounts. Money is "the great wheel of circulation," which effects the transfer of goods in process of production and the distribution of the finished goods to the consumers. It is an organ of the economic commonwealth rather than an expedient of accounting and a conventional repository of wealth. It is perhaps superfluous to remark that to the "plain man," who is not concerned with the "natural course of things" in a consummate Geldwirtschaft, the money that passes his hand is not a "great wheel of circulation." To the Samoyed, for instance, the reindeer which serves him as unit of value is wealth in the most concrete and tangible form. Much the same is true of coin, or even of bank-notes, in the apprehension of unsophisticated people among ourselves to-day. And yet it is in terms of the habits and conditions of life of these "plain people" that the development of money will have to be accounted for if it is to be stated in terms of cause and effect.

The few scattered passages already cited may serve to illustrate how Adam Smith's animistic or teleological bent shapes the general structure of his theory and gives it consistency. The principle of definitive formulation in Adam Smith's economic knowledge is afforded by a putative purpose that does not at any point enter causally into the economic life process which he seeks to know. This formative or normative purpose or end is not freely conceived to enter as an efficient agent in the events discussed, or to be in any way consciously present in the process. It can scarcely be taken as an animistic agency engaged in the process. It sanctions the course of things, and gives legitimacy and substance to the sequence of events, so far as this sequence may be made to square with the requirements of the imputed end. It has therefore a ceremonial or symbolical force only, and lends the discussion a ceremonial competency; although with economists who have been in passable agreement with

Adam Smith as regards the legitimate end of economic life this ceremonial consistency, or consistency de jure, has for many purposes been accepted as the formulation of a causal continuity in the phenomena that have been interpreted in its terms. Elucidations of what normally ought to happen, as a matter of ceremonial necessity, have in this way come to pass for an account of matters of fact.

But, as has already been pointed out, there is much more to Adam Smith's exposition of theory than a formulation of what ought to be. Much of the advance he achieved over his predecessors consists in a larger and more painstaking scrutiny of facts, and a more consistent tracing out of causal continuity in the facts handled. No doubt, his superiority over the Physiocrats, that characteristic of his work by virtue of which it superseded theirs in the farther growth of economic science, lies to some extent in his recourse to a different, more modern ground of normality,-- a ground more in consonance with the body of preconceptions that have had the vogue in later generations. It is a shifting of the point of view from which the facts are handled; but it comes in great part to a substitution of a new body of preconceptions for the old, or a new adaptation of the old ground of finality, rather than an elimination of all metaphysical or animistic norms of valuation. With Adam Smith, as with the Physiocrats, the fundamental question, the answer to which affords the point of departure and the norm of procedure, is a question of substantiality or economic "reality." With both, the answer to this question is given naively, as a deliverance of common sense. Neither is disturbed by doubts as to this deliverance of common sense or by any need of scrutinising it. To the Physiocrats this substantial ground of economic reality is the nutritive process of Nature. To Adam Smith it is Labor. His reality has the advantage of being the deliverance of the common sense of a more modern community, and one that has maintained itself in force more widely and in better consonance with the facts of latter-day industry. The Physiocrats owe their preconception of the productiveness of nature to the habits of thought of a community in whose economic life the dominant phenomenon was the owner of agricultural land. Adam Smith owes his preconception in favor of labor to a community in which the obtrusive economic feature of the immediate past was handicraft and agriculture, with commerce as a scarcely secondary phenomenon.

So far as Adam Smith's economic theories are a tracing out of the causal sequence in economic phenomena, they are worked out in terms given by these two main directions of activity, -- human effort directed to the shaping of the material means of life, and human effort and discretion directed to a pecuniary gain. The former is the great, substantial productive force: the latter is not immediately, or proximately, productive.(17*) Adam Smith still has too lively a sense of the nutritive purpose of the order of nature freely to extend the concept of productiveness to any activity that does not yield a material increase of the creature comforts. His instinctive appreciation of the substantial virtue of whatever effectually furthers nutrition, even leads him into the concession that "in agriculture nature labors along with man," although the general tenor of his argument is that the productive force with which the economist always has to count is human labor. This recognised substantiality of labor as productive is, as has already been remarked, accountable for his effort to reduce to terms of productive labor such a category of distribution as exchange value.

With but slight qualification, it will hold that, in the causal sequence which Adam Smith traces out in his economic theories proper (contained in the first three books of the Wealth of Nations), the causally efficient factor is conceived to be human nature in these two relations, -- of productive efficiency and pecuniary gain through exchange. Pecuniary gain -- gain in the material means of life through barter -- furnishes the motive force to the economic activity of the individual; although productive efficiency is the legitimate, normal end of the community's economic life. To such an extent does this concept of man's seeking his ends through "truck, barter, and exchange" pervade Adam Smith's treatment of economic processes that he even states production in its terms, and says that,, labor was the first price, the original purchase-money, that was paid for all things."(18*) The human nature engaged in this pecuniary traffic is conceived in somewhat hedonistic terms, and the motives and movements of men are normalised to fit the requirements of a hedonistically conceived order of nature. Men are very much alike in their native aptitudes and propensities;(19*) and, so far as economic theory need take account of these aptitudes and propensities, they are aptitudes for the production of the "necessaries and conveniences of life," and propensities to secure as great a share of these creature comforts as may be.

Adam Smith's conception of normal human nature -- that is to say, the human factor which enters causally in the process which economic theory discusses -- comes, on the whole, to this: Men exert their force and skill in a mechanical process of production, and their pecuniary sagacity in a competitive process of distribution, with a view to individual gain in the material means of life. These material means are sought in order to the satisfaction of men's natural wants through their consumption. It is true, much else enters into men's endeavors in the struggle for wealth, as Adam Smith points out; but this consumption comprises the legitimate range of incentives, and a theory which concerns itself with the natural course of things need take but incidental account of what does not come legitimately in the natural course. In point of fact, there are appreciable "actual," though scarcely "real," departures from this rule. They are spurious and insubstantial departures, and do not properly come within the purview of the stricter theory. And, since human nature is strikingly uniform, in Adam Smith's apprehension, both the efforts put forth and the consumptive effect accomplished may be put in quantitative terms and treated algebraically, with the result that the entire range of phenomena comprised under the head of consumption need be but incidentally considered; and the theory of production and distribution is complete when the goods or the values have been traced to their disappearance in the hands of their ultimate owners. The reflex effect of consumption upon production and distribution is, on the whole, quantitative only.

Adam Smith's preconception of a normal teleological order of procedure in the natural course, therefore, affects not only those features of theory where he is avowedly concerned with building up a normal scheme of the economic process. Through his normalising the chief causal factor engaged in the process, it affects also his arguments from cause to effect.(20*) What makes this latter feature worth particular attention is the fact that his successors carried this normalisation farther, and employed it with less frequent reference to the mitigating exceptions which Adam Smith notices by the way.

The reason for that farther and more consistent normalisation of human nature which gives us the "economic man" at the hands of Adam Smith's successors lies, in great part, in the utilitarian philosophy that entered in force and in consummate form at about the turning of the century. Some credit in the work of normalisation is due also to the farther supersession of handicraft by the "capitalistic" industry that came in at the same time and in pretty close relation with the utilitarian views.

After Adam Smith's day, economics fell into profane hands. Apart from Malthus, who, of all the greater economists, stands nearest to Adam Smith on such metaphysical heads as have an immediate bearing upon the premises of economic science, the next generation do not approach their subject from the point of view of a divinely instituted, order; nor do they discuss human interests with that gently optimistic spirit of submission that belongs to the economist who goes to his work with the fear of God before his eyes. Even with Malthus the recourse to the divinely sanctioned order of nature is somewhat sparing and temperate. But it is significant for the later course of economic theory that, while Malthus may well be accounted the truest continuer of Adam Smith, it was the undevout utilitarians that became the spokesmen of the science after Adam Smith's time.

There is no wide breach between Adam Smith and the utilitarians, either in details of doctrine or in the concrete conclusions arrived at as regards questions of policy. On these heads Adam Smith might well be classed as a moderate utilitarian, particularly so far as regards his economic work. Malthus has still more of a utilitarian air, -- so much so, indeed, that he is not infrequently spoken of as a utilitarian. This view, convincingly set forth by Mr. Bonar,(21*) is no doubt well borne out by a detailed scrutiny of Malthus's economic doctrines. His humanitarian bias is evident throughout, and his weakness for considerations of expediency is the great blemish of his scientific work. But, for all that, in order to an appreciation of the change that came over classical economics with the rise of Benthamism, it is necessary to note that the agreement in this matter between Adam Smith and the disciples of Bentham, and less decidedly that between Malthus and the latter, is a coincidence of conclusions rather than an identity of preconceptions.(22*)

With Adam Smith the ultimate ground of economic reality is the design of God, the teleological order; and his utilitarian generalisations, as well as the hedonistic character of his economic man, are but methods of the working out of this natural order, not the substantial and self-legitimating ground. Shifty as Malthus's metaphysics are, much the same is to be said for him.(23*) Of the utilitarians proper the converse is true, although here, again, there is by no means utter consistency The substantial economic ground is pleasure and pain: the teleological order (even the design of God, where that is admitted) is the method of its working-out.

It may be unnecessary here to go into the farther implications, psychological and ethical, which this preconception of the utilitarians involves. And even this much may seem a taking of excessive pains with a distinction that marks no tangible difference. But a reading of the classical doctrines, with something of this metaphysics of political economy in mind, will show how, and in great part why, the later economists of the classical line diverged from Adam Smith's tenets in the early years of the century, until it has been necessary to interpret Adam Smith somewhat shrewdly in order to save him from heresy.

The post-Bentham economics is substantially a theory of value. This is altogether the dominant feature of the body of doctrines; the rest follows from, or is adapted to, this central discipline. The doctrine of value is of very great importance also in Adam Smith; but Adam Smith's economics is a theory of the production and apportionment of the material, means of life.(24*) With Adam Smith, value is discussed from the point of view of production. With the utilitarians, production is discussed from the point of view of value. The former makes value an outcome of the process of production: the latter make production the outcome of a valuation process.

The point of departure with Adam Smith is the "productive power of labor." (25*) With Ricardo it is a pecuniary problem concerned in the distribution of ownership;(26*) but the classical writers are followers of Adam Smith, and improve upon and correct the results arrived at by him, and the difference of point of view, therefore, becomes evident in their divergence from him, and the different distribution of emphasis, rather than in a new and antagonistic departure.

The reason for this shifting of the center of gravity from production to valuation lies, proximately, in Bentham's revision of the "principles " of morals. Bentham's philosophical position is, of course, not a self-explanatory phenomenon, nor does the effect of Benthamism extend only to those who are avowed followers of Bentham; for Bentham is the exponent of a cultural change that affects the habits of thought of the entire community. The immediate point of Bentham's work, as affecting the habits of thought of the educated community, is the substitution of hedonism (utility) in place of achievement of purpose, as a ground of legitimacy and a guide in the normalisation of knowledge. Its effect is most patent in speculations on morals, where it inculcates determinism. Its close connection with determinism in ethics points the way to what may be expected of its working in economics. In both cases the result is that human action is construed in terms of the causal forces of the environment, the human agent being, at the best, taken as a mechanism of commutation, through the workings of which the sensuous effects wrought by the impinging forces of the environment are, by an enforced process of valuation, transmuted without quantitative discrepancy into moral or economic conduct, as the case may be. In ethics and economics alike the subject-matter of the theory is this valuation process that expresses itself in conduct, resulting, in the case of economic conduct, in the pursuit of the greatest gain or least sacrifice.

Metaphysically or cosmologically considered, the human nature into the motions of which hedonistic ethics and economics inquire is an intermediate term in a causal sequence, of which the initial and the terminal members are sensuous impressions and the details of conduct. This intermediate term conveys the sensuous impulse without loss of force to its eventuation in conduct. For the purpose of the valuation process through which the impulse is so conveyed, human nature may, therefore, be accepted as uniform; and the theory of the valuation process may be formulated quantitatively, in terms of the material forces affecting the human sensory and of their equivalents in the resulting activity. In the language of economics, the theory of value may be stated in terms of the consumable goods that afford the incentive to effort and the expenditure undergone in order to procure them. Between these two there subsists a necessary equality; but the magnitudes between which the equality subsists are hedonistic magnitudes, not magnitudes of kinetic energy nor of vital force, for the terms handled are sensuous terms. It is true, since human nature is substantially uniform, passive, and unalterable in respect of men's capacity for sensuous affection, there may also be presumed to subsist a substantial equality between the psychological effect to be wrought by the consumption of goods, on the one side, and the resulting expenditure of kinetic or vital force, on the other side; but such an equality is, after all, of the nature of a coincidence, although there should be a strong presumption in favor of its prevailing on an average and in the common run of cases. Hedonism, however, does not postulate uniformity between men except in the respect of sensuous cause and effect.

The theory of value which hedonism gives is, therefore, a theory of cost in terms of discomfort. By virtue of the hedonistic equilibrium reached through the valuation process, the sacrifice or expenditure of sensuous reality involved in acquisition is the equivalent of the sensuous gain secured. An alternative statement might perhaps be made, to the effect that the measure of the value of goods is not the sacrifice or discomfort undergone, but the sensuous gain that accrues from the acquisition of the goods; but this is plainly only an alternative statement, and there are special reasons in the economic life of the time why the statement in terms of cost, rather than in terms of "utility," should commend itself to the earlier classical economists.

On comparing the utilitarian doctrine of value with

earlier theories, then, the case stands somewhat as follows. The Physiocrats and Adam Smith contemplate value as a measure of the productive force that realises itself in the valuable article. With the Physiocrats this productive force is the "anabolism " of Nature (to resort to a physiological term): with Adam Smith it is chiefly human labor directed to heightening the serviceability of the materials with which it is occupied. Production causes value in either case. The post-Bentham economics contemplates value as a measure of, or as measured by the irksomeness of the effort involved in procuring the valuable goods. As Mr. E. C. K. Gonner has admirably pointed out,(27*) Ricardo -- and the like holds true of classical economics generally -- makes cost the foundation of value, not its cause. This resting of value on cost takes place through a valuation. Any one who will read Adam Smith's theoretical exposition to as good purpose as Mr. Gonner has read Ricardo will scarcely fail to find that the converse is true in Adam Smith's case. But the causal relation of cost to value holds only as regards "natural" or "real" value in Adam Smith's doctrine. As regards market price, Adam Smith's theory does not differ greatly from that of Ricardo on this head. He does not overlook the valuation process by which market price is adjusted and the course of investment is guided, and his discussion of this process runs in terms that should be acceptable to any hedonist.

The shifting of the point of view that comes into

economics with the acceptance of utilitarian ethics and its correlate, the associationist psychology, is in great part a shifting to the ground of causal sequence as contrasted with that of serviceability to a preconceived end. This is indicated even by the main fact already cited, -- that the utilitarian economists make exchange value the central feature of their theories, rather than the conduciveness of industry to the community's material welfare. Hedonistic exchange value is the outcome of a valuation process enforced by the apprehended pleasure-giving capacities of the items valued. And in the utilitarian theories of production, arrived at from the standpoint so given by exchange value, the conduciveness to welfare is not the objective point of the argument. This objective point is rather the bearing of productive enterprise upon the individual fortunes of the agents engaged, or upon the fortunes of the several distinguishable classes of beneficiaries comprised in the industrial community; for the great immediate bearing of exchange values upon the life of the collectivity is their bearing upon the distribution of wealth. Value is a category of distribution. The result is that, as is well shown by Mr. Cannan's discussion,(28*) the theories of production offered by the classical economists have been sensibly scant, and have been carried out with a constant view to the doctrines on distribution. An incidental but telling demonstration of the same facts is given by Professor Bucher; (29*) and in illustration may be cited Torrens's

Essay On the Production of Wealth, which is to a good extent occupied with discussions of value and distribution. The classical theories of production have been theories of the production of "wealth"; and "wealth," in classical usage, consists of material things having exchange value. During the vogue of the classical economics the accepted characteristic by which "wealth" has been defined has been its amenability to ownership. Neither in Adam Smith nor in the Physiocrats is this amenability to ownership made so much of, nor is it in a similar degree accepted as a definite mark of the subject-matter of the science.

As their hedonistic preconception would require, then, it is to the pecuniary side of life that the classical economists give their most serious attention, and it is the pecuniary bearing of any given phenomenon or of any institution that commonly shapes the issue of the argument. The causal sequence about which the discussion centers is a process of pecuniary valuation. It runs on distribution, ownership, acquisition, gain, investment, exchange.(30*) In this way the doctrines on production come to take a pecuniary coloring; as is seen in a less degree also in Adam Smith, and even in the Physiocrats, although these earlier economists very rarely, if ever, lose touch with the concept of generic serviceability as the characteristic feature of production. The tradition derived from Adam Smith, which made productivity and serviceability the substantial features of economic life, was not abruptly put aside by his successors, though the emphasis was differently distributed by them in following out the line of investigation to which the tradition pointed the way. In the classical economics the ideas of production and of acquisition are not commonly held apart, and very much of what passes for a theory of production is occupied with phenomena of investment and acquisition. Torrens's Essay is a case in point, though by no means an extreme case.

This is as it should be; for to the consistent hedonist the sole motive force concerned in the industrial process is the self-regarding motive of pecuniary gain, and industrial activity is but an intermediate term between the expenditure or discomfort undergone and the pecuniary gain sought. Whether the end and outcome is an invidious gain for the individual (in contrast with or at the cost of his neighbors), or an enhancement of the facility of human life on the whole, is altogether a by-question in any discussion of the range of incentives by which men are prompted to their work or the direction which their efforts take. The serviceability of the given line of activity, for the life purposes of the community or for one's neighbors, "is not of the essence of this contract." These features of serviceability come into the account chiefly as affecting the vendibility of what the given individual has to offer in seeking gain through a bargain.(31*)

In hedonistic theory the substantial end of economic life is individual, gain, and for this purpose production and acquisition may be taken as fairly coincident, if not identical. Moreover, society, in the utilitarian philosophy, is the algebraic sum of the individuals; and the interest of the society is the sum of the interests of the individuals. It follows by easy consequence, whether strictly true or not, that the sum of individual gains is the gain of the society, and that, in serving his own interest in the way of acquisition, the individual serves the collective interest of the community. Productivity or serviceability is, therefore, to be presumed of any occupation or enterprise that looks to a pecuniary gain; and so, by a roundabout path, we get back to the ancient conclusion of Adam Smith, that the remuneration of classes or persons engaged in industry coincides with their productive contribution to the output of services and consumable goods.

A felicitous illustration of the working of this hedonistic norm in classical economic doctrine is afforded by the theory of the wages of superintendence, -- an element in distribution which is not much more than suggested in Adam Smith, but which receives ampler and more painstaking attention as the classical body of doctrines reaches a fuller development. The "wages of superintendence" are the gains due to pecuniary management. They are the gains that come to the director of the,, business," -- not those that go to the director of the mechanical process or to the foreman of the shop. The latter are wages simply. This distinction is not altogether clear in the earlier writers, but it is clearly enough contained in the fuller development of the theory.

The undertaker's work is the management of investment. It is altogether of a pecuniary character, and its proximate aim is "the main chance." If it leads, indirectly, to an enhancement of serviceability or a heightened aggregate output of consumable goods, that is a fortuitous circumstance incident to that heightened vendibility on which the investor's gain depends. Yet the classical doctrine says frankly that the wages of superintendence are the remuneration of superior productivity,(32*) and the classical theory of production is in good part a doctrine of investment in which the identity of production and pecuniary gain is taken for granted.

The substitution of investment in the place of industry as the central and substantial fact in the process of production is due not to the acceptance of hedonism simply, but rather to the conjunction of hedonism with an economic situation of which the investment of capital and its management for gain was the most obvious feature. The situation which shaped the common-sense apprehension of economic facts at the time was what has since been called a capitalistic system, in which pecuniary enterprise and the phenomena of the market were the dominant and tone-giving facts. But this economic situation was also the chief ground for the vogue of hedonism in economics; so that hedonistic economics may be taken as an interpretation of human nature in terms of the market-place. The market and the "business world," to which the business man in his pursuit of gain was required to adapt his motives, had by this time grown so large that the course of business events was beyond the control of any one person; and at the same time those far-reaching organisations of invested wealth which have latterly come to prevail and to coerce the market were not then in the foreground. The course of market events took its passionless way without traceable relation or deference to any man's convenience and without traceable guidance towards an ulterior end. Man's part in this pecuniary world was to respond with alacrity to the situation, and so adapt his vendible effects to the shifting demand as to realise something in the outcome. What he gained in his traffic was gained without loss to those with whom he dealt, for they paid no more than the goods were worth to them. One man's gain need not be another's loss; and, if it is not, then it is net gain to the community.

Among the striking remoter effects of the hedonistic preconception, and its working out in terms of pecuniary gain, is the classical failure to discriminate between capital as investment and capital as industrial appliances. This is, of course, closely related to the point already spoken of. The appliances of industry further the production of goods, therefore capital (invested wealth) is productive; and the rate of its average remuneration marks the degree of its productiveness.(33*) The most obvious fact limiting the pecuniary gain secured by means of invested wealth is the sum invested. Therefore, capital limits the productiveness of industry; and the chief and indispensable condition to an advance in material well-being is the accumulation of invested wealth. In discussing the conditions of industrial improvement, it is usual to assume that "the state of the arts remains unchanged," which is, for all purposes but that of a doctrine of profits per cent., an exclusion of the main fact. Investments may, further, be transferred from one enterprise to another. Therefore, and in that degree, the means of production are "mobile."

Under the hands of the great utilitarian writers, therefore, political economy is developed into a science of wealth, taking that term in the pecuniary sense, as things amenable to ownership. The course of things in economic life is treated as a sequence of pecuniary events, and economic theory becomes a theory of what should happen in that consummate situation where the permutation of pecuniary magnitudes takes place without disturbance and without retardation. In this consummate situation the pecuniary motive has its perfect work, and guides all the acts of economic man in a guileless, colorless, unswerving quest of the greatest gain at the least sacrifice. Of course, this perfect competitive system, with its untainted "economic man,"is a feat of scientific imagination, and is not intended as a competent expression of fact. It is an expedient of abstract reasoning; and its avowed competency extends only to the abstract principles, the fundamental laws of the science, which hold only so far as the abstraction holds. But, as happens in such cases, having once been accepted and assimilated as real, though perhaps not as actual, it becomes an effective constituent in the inquirer's habits of thought, and goes to shape his knowledge of facts. It comes to serve as a norm of substantiality or legitimacy; and facts in some degree fall under its constraint, as is exemplified by many allegations regarding the "tendency" of things.

To this consummation, which Senior speaks of as "the natural state of man,"(34*) human development tends by force of the hedonistic character of human nature; and in terms of its approximation to this natural state, therefore, the immature actual situation had best be stated. The pure theory, the "hypothetical science" of Cairnes, "traces the phenomena of the production and distribution of wealth up to their causes, in the principles of human nature and the laws and events -- physical, political, and social -- of the external world."(35*) But since the principles of human nature that give the outcome in men's economic conduct, so far as it touches the production and distribution of wealth, are but the simple and constant sequence of hedonistic cause and effect, the element of human nature may fairly be eliminated from the problem, with great gain in simplicity and expedition. Human nature being eliminated, as being a constant intermediate term, and all institutional features of the situation being also eliminated (as being similar constants under that natural or consummate pecuniary regime with which the pure theory is concerned), the laws of the phenomena of wealth may be formulated in terms of the remaining factors. These factors are the vendible items that men handle in these processes of production and distribution and economic laws come, therefore, to be expressions of the algebraic relations subsisting between the various elements of wealth and investment, -- capital, labor, land, supply and demand of one and the other, profits, interest, wages. Even such items as credit and population become dissociated from the personal factor, and figure in the computation as elemental factors acting and reacting though a permutation of values over the heads of the good people whose welfare they are working out.

To sum up: the classical economics, having primarily to do with the pecuniary side of life, is a theory of a process of valuation. But since the human nature at whose hands and for whose behoof the valuation takes place is simple and constant in its reaction to pecuniary stimulus, and since no other feature of human nature is legitimately present in economic phenomena than this reaction to pecuniary stimulus, the valuer concerned in the matter is to be overlooked or eliminated; and the theory of the valuation process then becomes a theory of the pecuniary interaction of the facts valued. It is a theory of valuation with the element of valuation left out,-- a theory of life stated in terms of the normal paraphernalia of life.

In the preconceptions with which classical economics set out were comprised the remnants of natural rights and of the order of nature, infused with that peculiarly mechanical natural theology that made its way into popular vogue on British ground during the eighteenth century and was reduced to a neutral tone by the British penchant for the commonplace -- stronger at this time than at any earlier period. The reason for this growing penchant for the commonplace, for the explanation of things in causal terms, lies partly in the growing resort to mechanical processes and mechanical prime movers in industry, partly in the (consequent) continued decline of the aristocracy and the priesthood, and partly in the growing density of population and the consequent greater specialisation and wider organisation of trade and business. The spread of the discipline of the natural sciences, largely incident to the mechanical industry, counts in the same direction; and obscurer factors in modern culture may have had their share.

The animistic preconception was not lost, but it lost tone; and it partly fell into abeyance, particularly so far as regards its avowal. It is visible chiefly in the unavowed readiness of the classical writers to accept as imminent and definitive any possible outcome which the writer's habit or temperament inclined him to accept as right and good. Hence the visible inclination of classical economists to a doctrine of the harmony of interests, and their somewhat uncircumspect readiness to state their generalisations in terms of what ought to happen according to the ideal requirements of that consummate Geldwirtschaft to which men "are impelled by the provisions of nature." (36*) By virtue of their hedonistic preconceptions, their habituation to the ways of a pecuniary culture, and their unavowed animistic faith that nature is in the right, the classical economists knew that the consummation to which, in the nature of things, all things tend, is the frictionless and beneficent competitive system. This competitive ideal, therefore, affords the normal, and conformity to its requirements affords the test of absolute economic truth. The standpoint so gained selectively guides the attention of the classical writers in their observation and apprehension of facts, and they come to see evidence of conformity or approach to the normal in the most unlikely places. Their observation is, in great part, interpretative, as observation commonly is. What is peculiar to the classical economists in this respect is their particular norm of procedure in the work of interpretation. And, by virtue of having achieved a standpoint of absolute economic normality, they became a "deductive" school, so called, in spite of the patent fact that they were pretty consistently employed with an inquiry into the causal sequence of economic phenomena.

The generalisation of observed facts becomes a normalisation of them, a statement of the phenomena in terms of their coincidence with, or divergence from, that normal tendency that makes for the actualisation of the absolute economic reality. This absolute or definitive ground of economic legitimacy lies beyond the causal sequence in which the observed phenomena are conceived to be interlinked. It is related to the concrete facts neither as cause nor as effect in any such way that the causal relation may be traced in a concrete instance. It has little causally to do either with the "mental" or with the "physical" data with which the classical economist is avowedly employed. Its relation to the process under discussion is that of an extraneous -- that is to say, a ceremonial -- legitimation. The body of knowledge gained by its help and under its guidance is, therefore, a taxonomic science.

So, by way of a concluding illustration, it may be pointed out that money, for instance, is normalised in terms of the legitimate economic tendency. It becomes a measure of value and a medium of exchange. It has become primarily an instrument of pecuniary commutation, instead of being, as under the earlier normalisation of Adam Smith, primarily a great wheel of circulation for the diffusion of consumable goods. The terms in which the laws of money, as of the other phenomena of pecuniary life, are formulated, are terms which connote its normal function in the life history of objective values as they live and move and have their being in the consummate pecuniary situation of the "natural" state. To a similar work of normalisation we owe those creatures of the myth-maker, the quantity theory and the wages-fund.

NOTES:

1. Bonar, Philosophy and Political Economy, pp. 177, 178.

2. "Every individual is continually exerting himself to find out the most advantageous employment for whatever capital he can command. It is his own advantage, and not that of the society, which he has in view. But the study of his own advantage naturally, or rather necessarily, leads him to prefer that employment which is most advantageous to the society... By directing that industry in such a manner as its produce may be of the greatest value, he intends only his own gain; and he is in this, as in many other cases, led by an invisible hand to promote an end which was no part of his intention. Nor is it always the worse for society that it was no part of it. By pursuing his own interest he

frequently promotes that of the society more effectually than when he really intends to promote it." Wealth of Nations, Book IV, chap. ii.

3. The discrepancy between the actual, causally determined situation and the divinely intended consummation is the metaphysical ground of all that inculcation of morality and enlightened policy that makes up so large a part of Adam Smith's work. The like, of course, holds true for all moralists and reformers who proceed on the assumption of a providential order.

4. "In the political body, however, the wisdom of nature has fortunately made ample provision for remedying many of the bad effects of the folly and injustice of man; in the same manner as it has done in the natural body, for remedying those of his sloth and intemperance." Wealth of Nations, Book IV, chap. ix.

5. E.g., "the real measure of the exchangeable value of all commodities." Wealth of Nations, Book I, chap. v, and repeatedly in the like connection.

6. E.g., Book I, chap. vii: "When the price of any commodity is neither more nor less than what is sufficient to pay the rent of the land, the wages of the

labor, and the profits of the stock employed in raising, preparing, and bringing it to market, according to their natural rates, the commodity is then sold for what may be called its natural price." "The actual price at which any commodity is commonly sold is called its market price. It may be either above or below or exactly the same with its natural price."

7. Lectures of Adam Smith (Ed. Cannan, 1896). p. 169.

8. "This division of labor, from which so many advantages are derived, is not originally the effect of any human wisdom, which foresees and intends that general opulence to which it gives occasion. It is the necessary though very slow and gradual consequence of a certain propensity in human nature which has in view no such extensive utility, -- the propensity to truck, barter, and exchange one thing for another. Whether this propensity be one of those original principles in human nature of which no further account can be given, or whether, as seems more probable, it be the necessary consequence of the faculties of reason and speech, it belongs not to our present subject to inquire." Wealth of Nations, Book I, chap. ii.

9. Wealth of Nations, Book I, chaps. v.-vii.

10. Wealth of Nations, Book I, chap. v.

11. As e.g., the entire discussion of the determination of Wages, Profits and Rent, in Book I, chaps. viii.-xi.

12. "There is in every society or neighborhood an ordinary or average rate both of wages and profit in every different employment of labor and stock. The rate is naturally regulated... partly by the general circumstance of the society... There is, likewise, in every socity or neighborhood an ordinary or average rate of rent, which is regulated, too... These ordinary or average rates may be called the natural rates of wages, profit, and rent, at the time and place in which they commonly prevail. When the price of any commodity is neither more nor less than what is sufficient to pay the rent of the land, the wages of the labor, and the profits of the stock employed in raising, preparing, and bringing it to market, according to their natural rates, the commodity is then sold for what may be called its natural price." Wealth of Nations, Book I, chap. vii.

13. "Such commodities may continue for whole centuries together to be sold at this high price; and that part of it which resolves itself into the rent of land is, in this case, the part which is generally paid above its

natural rate." Book I, chap. vii.

14. Wealth of Nations, Book I, chap. vi; also chap. viii.

15. For an instance of how these early phases of industrial development appear, when not seen in the light of Adam Smith's preconception, see, among others, Bucher, Entstehung der Volkswirtschagt.

16. Book I, chap. iv.

17. See Wealth of Nations, Book II, chap. v, "Of the Different Employment of Capitals."

18. Wealth of Nations, Book I, chap. v. See also the plea for free trade, Book IV, chap. ii: "But the annual revenue of every society is always precisely equal to the exchangeable value of the whole annual produce of its industry, or, rather, is precisely the same thing with that exchangeable value."

19. "The difference of natural talents in different men is in reality much less than we are aware of." Wealth of Nations, Book I, chap. ii.

20. "Mit diesen philosophischen Ueberzeugungen tritt

nun Adam Smith an die Welf der Engahrung heran, and es ergiebt sich ihm die Richtigkeit der Principien. Der Reiz der Smiths'schen Schriften beruht zum grossen Teile darauf, dass Smith die Principien in so innige Verbindung mit dem Thatsachlichen gebracht. Hie und da werden dann auch die Principien, was durch diese Verbindung veranlasst wird, an ihren Spitzen etwas algeschliffen, ihre allruscharfe Auspragung dadurch vermieden. Nichtsdestoweniger aber bleiben sie stets die leitenden Grundgedanken." Richard Zeyss, Adam Smith und der Eigennutz (Tubingen, 1889), p. 110.

21. See, e.g., Malthus and his Work, especially Book III, as also the chapter on Malthus in Philosophy and Political Economy, Book III, Modern Philosophy: Utilitarian Economics, chap. i, "Malthus." 22. Ricardo is here taken as a utilitarian of the Benthamite color, although he cannot be classed as a disciple of Bentham. His hedonism is but the uncritically accepted metaphysics comprised in the common sense of his time, and his substantial coincidence with Bentham goes to show how well diffused the hedonist preconception was at the time.

23. Cf. Bonar, Malthus and his Work, pp. 323-336.

24. His work is an inquiry into "the Nature and Causes of the Wealth of Nations."

25. "The annual labor of every nation is the fund which originally supplies it with all the necessaries and conveniences of life which it annually consumes, and which consist always either in the immediate produce of that labor or in what is purchases with that produce from other nations." Wealth of Nations, "Introduction and Plan," opening paragraph.

26. "The produce of the earth -- all that is derived from its surface by the united application of labor, machinery and capital -- is divided among three classes of the community... To determine the laws which regulate this distribution is the principal problem of political economy." Political Economy, Preface.

27. In the introductory essay to his edition of Ricardo's Political Economy. See, e.g., paragraphs 9 and 24.

28. Theories of Production and Distribution, 1776-1848.

29. Entstehung der Volkswirtschaft (second edition). Cf. especially chaps. ii, iii, vi, and vii.

30. "Even if we put aside all questions which involve a consideration of the effects of industrial institutions in modifying the habits and character of the classes of the community... that enough still remains to constitute a separate science, the mere enumeration of the chief terms of economics -- wealth, value, exchange, credit, money, capital, and commodity -- will suffice to show." Shirres, Analysis of the Ideas of Economics (London, 1893), pp. 8 and 9.

31. "If a commodity were in no way useful... it would be destitute of exchangeable value;... (but), possessing utility, commodities derive their exchangeable value from two sources," etc. Ricardo, Political Economy, chap. i, sect I.

32. Cf., for instance, Senior, Political Economy (London, 1872), particularly pp. 88, 89, and 130-135, where the wages of superintendence are, somewhat reluctantly, classed under profits; and the work of superintendence is thereupon conceived as being, immediately or remotely, an exercise of "abstinence" and a productive work. The illustration of the bill-broker is particularly apt. The like view of the wages of superintendence in an article of theory with more than one of the later descendents of the classical line.

33. Cf. Bohm-Bawerk, Capital and Interest, Books II and IV, as well as the Introduction and chaps. iv and v of Book I. Bohm-Bawerk's discussion bears less immediately on the present point than the similarity of the terms employed would suggest.

34. Political Economy, p. 87.

35. Character and Logical Method of Political Economy (New York, 1875), p. 71. Cairnes may not be altogether representative of the high tide of classicism, but his characterisation of the science is none the less to the point.

36. Senior, Political Economy, p. 87.

THE PRECONCEPTIONS OF ECONOMIC SCIENCE,

III

Thorstein Veblen
The Quarterly Journal of Economics, volume 14, 1900.

IN what has already been said, it has appeared that the changes which have supervened in the preconceptions of the earlier economists constitute a somewhat orderly succession. The feature of chief interest in this development has been a gradual change in the received grounds of finality to which the successive generations of economists have brought their theoretical output, on which they have been content to rest their conclusions, and beyond which they have not been moved to push their analysis of events or their scrutiny of phenomena. There has been a fairly unbroken sequence of development in what may be called the canons of economic reality; or, to put it in other words, there has been a precession of the point of view from which facts have been handled and valued for the purpose of economic science.

The notion which has in its time prevailed so widely, that there is in the sequence of events a consistent trend which it is the office of the science to ascertain and turn to account, -- this notion may be well founded or not. But that there is something of such a consistent trend in the sequence of the canons of knowledge under whose guidance the scientist works is not only a generalisation from the past course of things, but lies in the nature of the case; for the canons of knowledge are of the nature of habits of thought, and habit does not break with the past, nor do the hereditary aptitudes that find expression in habit vary gratuitously with the mere lapse of time. What is true in this respect, for instance, in the domain of law and institutions is true, likewise, in the domain of science. What men have learned to accept as good and definitive for the guidance of conduct and of human relations remains true and definitive and unimpeachable until the exigencies of a later, altered situation enforce a variation from the norms and canons of the past, and so give rise to a modification of the habits of thought that decide what is, for the time, right in human conduct. So in good and science the ancient ground of finality remains a valid test of scientific truth until the altered exigencies of later life enforce habits of thought that are not wholly in consonance with the received notions as to what constitutes the ultimate, self-legitimating term -- the substantial reality -- to which knowledge in any given case must penetrate.

This ultimate term or ground of knowledge is always of a metaphysical character. It is something in the way of a preconception, accepted uncritically, but applied in criticism and demonstration of all else with which the science is concerned. So soon as it comes to be criticised, it is in a way to be superseded by a new, more or less altered formulation; for criticism of it means that it is no longer fit to survive unaltered in the altered complex of habits of thought to which it is called upon to serve as fundamental principle. It is subject to natural selection and selective adaptation, as are other conventions. The underlying metaphysics of scientific research and purpose, therefore, changes gradually and, of course, incompletely, much as is the case with the metaphysics underlying the common law and the schedule of civil rights. As in the legal framework the now avowedly useless and meaningless preconceptions of status and caste and precedent are even yet at the most metamorphosed and obsolescent rather than overpassed, -- witness the facts of inheritance, vested interests, the outlawry of debts through lapse of time, the competence of the State to coerce individuals into support of a given, policy -- so in the science the living generation has not seen an abrupt and traceless disappearance of the metaphysics that fixed the point of view of the early classical political economy. This is true even for those groups of economists who have most incontinently protested against the absurdity of the classical doctrines and methods. In Professor Marshall's words, "There has been no real breach of continuity in the development of the science,"

But, while there has been no breach, there has none the less been change, -- more far-reaching change than some of us are glad to recognise; for who would not be glad to read his own modern views into the convincing words of the great masters?

Seen through modern eyes and without effort to turn past gains to modern account, the metaphysical or preconceptional furniture of political economy as it stood about the middle of this century may come to look quite curious. The two main canons of truth on which the science proceeded, and with which the inquiry is here concerned, were: (a) a hedonistic -associational psychology, and (b) an uncritical conviction that there is a meliorative trend in the course of events, apart from the conscious ends of the individual members of the community. This axiom of a meliorative developmental trend fell into shape as a belief in an organic or quasi-organic (physiological)(1*) life process on the part of the economic community or of the nation; and this belief carried with it something of a constraining sense of self realising cycles of growth, maturity and decay in the life history of nations or communities.

Neglecting what may for the immediate purpose be negligible in this outline of fundamental tenets, it will bear the following construction. (a) On the ground of the hedonistic or associational psychology, all spiritual continuity and any consequent teleological trend is tacitly denied so far as regards individual conduct, where the later psychology, and the sciences which build on this later psychology, insist upon and find such a teleological trend at every turn. (b) Such a spiritual or quasi-spiritual continuity and teleological trend is uncritically affirmed as regards the non-human sequence or the sequence of events in the affairs of collective life, where the modern sciences diligently assert that nothing of the kind is discernible, or that, if it is discernible, its recognition is beside the point, so far as concerns the purposes of the science.

This position, here outlined with as little qualification as may be admissible, embodies the general metaphysical ground of that classical political economy that affords the point of departure for Mill and Cairnes, and also for Jevons. And what is to be said of Mill and Cairnes in this connection will apply to the later course of the science, though with a gradually lessening force. `By the middle of the century the psychological premises of the science are no longer so neat and succinct as they were in the days of Bentham and James Mill. At J.S. Mill's hands. for instance, the naively quantitative hedonism of Bentham is being supplanted by a sophisticated hedonism, which makes much of an assumed qualitative divergence between the different kinds of pleasures that afford the motives of conduct. This revision of hedonistic dogma, of course, means a departure from the strict hedonistic ground. Correlated with this advance more closely in the substance of the change than in the assignable dates, is a concomitant improvement -- at least, set forth as an improvement -- upon the received associational psychology, whereby "similarity" is brought in to supplement "contiguity" as a ground of connection between ideas. This change is well shown in the work of J.S. Mill and Bain. In spite of all the ingenuity spent in maintaining the associational legitimacy of this new article of theory, it remains a patent innovation and a departure from the ancient standpoint. As is true of the improved hedonism, so it is true of the new theory of association that it is no longer able to construe the process which it discusses as a purely mechanical process, a concatenation of items simply. Similarity of impressions implies a comparison of impressions by the mind in which the association takes place, and thereby it implies some degree of constructive work on the part of the perceiving subject. The perceiver is thereby construed to be an agent in the work of perception; therefore, he must be possessed of a point of view and an end dominating the perceptive process. To perceive the similarity, he must be guided by an interest in the outcome, and must "attend," The like applies to the introduction of qualitative distinctions into the hedonistic theory of conduct. Apperception in the one case and discretion in the other cease to be the mere registration of a simple and personally uncolored sequence of permutations enforced by

the factors of the external world. There is implied a spiritual
-- that is to say, active -- "teleological" continuity of process
on the part of the perceiving or of the discretionary agent,
as the case may be.

It is on the ground of their departure from the stricter
hedonistic premises that Mill and, after him, Cairnes are
able, for instance, to offer their improvement upon the earlier
doctrine of cost of production as determining value. Since
it is conceived that the motives which guide men in their
choice of employments and of domicile differ from man to
man and from class to class, not only in degree, but in kind,
and since varying antecedents, of heredity and of habit,
variously influence men in their choice of a manner of life,
therefore the mere quantitative pecuniary stimulus cannot
be depended on to decide the outcome without recourse.
There are determinable variations in the alacrity with which
different classes or communities respond to the pecuniary
stimulus; and in so far as this condition prevails, the classes
or communities in question are non-competing. Between
such non-competing groups the norm that determines values
is not the unmitigated norm of cost of production taken
absolutely, but only taken relatively. The formula of cost of
production is therefore modified into a formula of reciprocal
demand. This revision of the cost-of-production doctrine is
extended only sparingly, and the emphasis is thrown on the
pecuniary circumstances on which depend the formation and

maintenance of non-competing groups. Consistency with the earlier teaching is carefully maintained, so far as may be; but extra-pecuniary factors are, after all, even if reluctantly, admitted into the body of the theory. So also, since there are higher and lower motives, higher and lower pleasures, -- as well as motives differing in degree, -- it follows that an unguided response even to the mere quantitative pecuniary stimuli may take different directions, and so may result in activities of widely differing outcome. Since activities set up in this way through appeal to higher and lower motives are no longer conceived to represent simply a mechanically adequate effect of the stimuli, working under the control of natural laws that tend to one beneficent consummation, therefore the outcome of activity set up even by the normal pecuniary stimuli may take a form that may or may not be serviceable to the community. Hence laissez-faire ceases to be a sure remedy for the ills of society. Human interests are still conceived normally to be at one; but the detail of individual conduct need not, therefore, necessarily serve these generic human interests.(2*) Therefore, other inducements than the unmitigated impact of pecuniary exigencies may be necessary to bring about a coincidence of class or individual endeavor with the interests of the community. It becomes incumbent on the advocate of laissez-faire to "prove his minor premise." It is no longer self-evident that:" Interests left to themselves tend to harmonious combinations, and to the progressive preponderance of the general good." (3*)

The natural-rights preconception begins to fall away as soon as the hedonistic mechanics have been seriously tampered with. Fact and right cease to coincide, because the individual in whom the rights are conceived to inhere has come to be something more than the field of intersection of natural forces that work out in human conduct. The mechanics of natural liberty -- that assumed constitution of things by force of which the free hedonistic play of the laws of nature across the open field of individual choice is sure to reach the right outcome -- is the hedonistic psychology, and the passing of the doctrine of natural rights and natural liberty whether as a premise or as a dogma, therefore coincides with the passing of that mechanics of conduct on the validity of which the theoretical acceptance of the dogma depends. It is, therefore, something more than a coincidence that the half-century which has seen the disintegration of the hedonistic faith and of the associational psychology has also seen the dissipation, in scientific speculations, of the concomitant faith in natural rights and in that benign order of nature of which the natural-rights dogma is a corollary.

It is, of course, not hereby intended to say that the later psychological views and premises imply a less close dependence of conduct on environment than do the earlier ones. Indeed, the reverse may well be held to be true. The pervading characteristic of later thinking is the constant recourse to a detailed analysis of phenomena in causal terms. The modern catchword, in the present connection, is" response to stimulus,' '. but the manner in which this response is conceived has changed. The fact, and ultimately the amplitude, at least in great part, of the reaction to stimulus, is conditioned by the forces in impact; but the constitution of the organism, as well as its attitude at the moment of impact, in great part decides what will serve as a stimulus, as well as what the manner and direction of the response will be.

The later psychology is biological, as contrasted with the metaphysical psychology of hedonism. It does not conceive the organism as a causal hiatus. The causal sequence in the "reflex arc" is, no doubt, continuous; but the continuity is not, as formerly, conceived in terms of spiritual substance transmitting a shock: it is conceived in terms of the life activity of the organism. Human conduct, taken as the reaction of such an organism under stimulus, may be stated in terms of tropism, involving, of course, a very close-knit causal sequence between the impact and the response, but at the same time imputing to the organism a habit of life and a self-directing and selective attention in meeting the complex of forces that make up its environment. The selective play of this tropismatic complex that constitutes the organism's habit of life under the impact of the forces of the environment counts as discretion.

So far, therefore, as it is to be placed in contrast with the hedonistic phase of the older psychological doctrines, the characteristic feature of the newer conception is the recognition of a selectively self-directing life process in the agent. While hedonism seeks the causal determinant of conduct in the (probable) outcome of action, the later conception seeks this determinant in the complex of propensities that constitutes man a functioning agent, that is to say, a personality. Instead of pleasure ultimately determining what human conduct shall be, the tropismatic propensities that eventuate in conduct ultimately determine what shall be pleasurable. For the purpose in hand, the consequence of the transition to the altered conception of human nature and its relation to the environment is that the newer view formulates conduct in terms of personality, whereas the earlier view was content to formulate it in terms of its provocation and its by-product. Therefore, for the sake of brevity, the older preconceptions of the science are here spoken of as construing human nature in inert terms, as contrasted with the newer, which construes it in terms of functioning.

It has already appeared above that the second great article of the metaphysics of classical political economy the belief in a meliorative trend or a benign order of nature -- is closely connected with the hedonistic conception of human nature; but this connection is more intimate and organic than appears from what has been said above. The two are so related as to stand or fall together, for the latter is but the obverse of the former. The doctrine of a trend in events imputes purpose to the sequence of events; that is, it invests this sequence with a discretionary, teleological character, which asserts itself in a constraint over all the steps in the sequence by which the supposed objective point is reached. But discretion touching a given end must be single, and must alone cover all the acts by which the end is to be reached. Therefore, no discretion resides in the intermediate terms through which the end is worked out. Therefore, man being such an intermediate term, discretion cannot be imputed to him without violating the supposition. Therefore, given an indefeasible meliorative trend in events, man is but a mechanical intermediary in the sequence. It is as such a mechanical intermediate term that the stricter hedonism construes human nature.(4*) Accordingly, when more of teleological activity came to be imputed to man, less was thereby allowed to the complex of events. Or it may be put in the converse form: When less of a teleological continuity came to be imputed to the course of events, more was thereby imputed to man's life process. The latter form of statement probably suggests the direction in which the causal relation runs, more nearly than the former. The change whereby the two metaphysical premises in question have lost their earlier force and symmetry, therefore, amounts to a (partial) shifting of the seat of putative personality from inanimate phenomena to man.

It may be mentioned in passing, as a detail lying perhaps afield, yet not devoid of significance for latter-day economic speculation, that this elimination of personality, and so of teleological content, from the sequence of events, and its increasing imputation to the conduct of the human agent, is incident to a growing resort to an apprehension of phenomena in terms of process rather than in terms of outcome, as was the habit in earlier schemes of knowledge. On this account the categories employed are, in a gradually increasing degree, categories of process, -- "dynamic" categories. But categories of process applied to conduct, to discretionary action, are teleological categories: whereas categories of process applied in the case of a sequence where the members of the sequence are not conceived to be charged with discretion, are, by the force of this conception itself, non-teleological, quantitative categories. The continuity comprised in the concept of process as applied to conduct is consequently a spiritual, teleological continuity. whereas the concept of process under the second head, the non-teleological sequence, comprises a continuity of a quantitative, causal kind, substantially the conservation of energy. In its turn the growing resort to categories of process in the formulation of knowledge is probably due to the epistemological discipline of modern mechanical industry, the technological exigencies of which enforce a constant recourse to the apprehension of phenomena in terms of process, differing therein from the earlier forms of industry, which neither obtruded visible mechanical process so constantly upon the apprehension nor so imperatively demanded an articulate recognition of continuity in the processes actually involved. The contrast in this respect is still more pronounced between the discipline of modern life in an industrial community and the discipline of life under the conventions of status and exploit that formerly prevailed.

To return to the benign order of nature, or the meliorative trend, -- its passing, as an article of economic faith, was not due to criticism leveled against it by the later classical economists on grounds of its epistemological incongruity. It was tried on its merits, as an alleged account of facts; and the weight of evidence went against it. The belief in a self-realising trend bad no sooner reached a competent and exhaustive statement -- e.g., at Bastiat's hands, as a dogma of the harmony of interests specifically applicable to the details of economic life than it began to lose ground. With his usual concision and incisiveness, Cairnes completed the destruction of Bastiat's special dogma, and put it forever beyond a rehearing. But Cairnes is not a destructive critic of the classical political economy, at least not in intention: he is an interpreter and continuer -- perhaps altogether the clearest and truest continuer -- of the classical teaching.

While he confuted Bastiat and discredited Bastiat's peculiar dogma, he did not thereby put the order of nature bodily out of the science. He qualified and improved it, very much as Mill qualified and improved the tenets of the hedonistic psychology. As Mill and the ethical speculation of his generation threw more of personality into the hedonistic psychology, so Cairnes and the speculators on scientific method (such as Mill and Jevons) attenuated the imputation of personality or teleological content to the process of material cause and effect. The work is of course, by no means, an achievement of Cairnes alone; but he is, perhaps, the best exponent of this advance in economic theory. In Cairnes's redaction this foundation of the science became the concept of a colorless normality. It was in Cairnes's time the fashion for speculators in other fields than the physical sciences to look to those sciences for guidance in method and for legitimation of the ideals of scientific theory which they were at work to realize. More than that, the large and fruitful achievements of the physical sciences had so far taken men's attention captive as to give an almost instinctive predilection for the methods that had approved themselves in that field. The ways of thinking which had on this ground become familiar to all scholars occupied with any scientific inquiry, had permeated their thinking on any subject whatever. This is eminently true of British thinking.

It had come to be a commonplace of the physical

sciences that "natural laws" are of the nature of empirical generalisations simply, or even of the nature of arithmetical averages. Even the underlying preconception of the modern physical sciences -- the law of the conservation of energy, or persistence of quantity -- was claimed to be an empirical generalisation, arrived at inductively and verified by experiment. It is true the alleged proof of the law took the whole conclusion for granted at the start, and used it constantly as a tacit axiom at every step in the argument which was to establish its truth; but that fact serves rather to emphasise than to call in question the abiding faith which these empiricists had in the sole efficacy of empirical generalisation. Had they been able overtly to admit any other than an associational origin of knowledge, they would have seen the impossibility of accounting on the mechanical grounds of association for the premise on which a;l experience of mechanical fact rests. That any other than a mechanical origin should be assigned to experience, or that any other than a so-conceived empirical ground was to be admitted for any general principle, was incompatible with the prejudices of men trained in the school of the associational psychology, however widely they perforce departed from this ideal in practice. Nothing of the nature of a personal element was to be admitted into these fundamental empirical generalisations; and nothing, therefore, of the nature of a discretionary or teleological movement was to be comprised in the generalisations to be accepted as" natural laws." Natural laws must in no degree be imbued with personality, must say nothing of an ulterior end; but for all that they remained "laws" of the sequences subsumed under them. So far is the reduction to colorless terms carried by Mill, for instance, that he formulates the natural laws as empirically ascertained sequences simply, even excluding or avoiding all imputation of causal continuity, as that term is commonly understood by the unsophisticated. In Mill's ideal no more of organic connection or continuity between the members of a sequence is implied in subsuming them under a law of causal relationship than is given by the ampersand, He is busied with dynamic sequences, but he persistently confines himself to static terms.

Under the guidance of the associational psychology, therefore, the extreme of discontinuity in the deliverances of inductive research is aimed at by those economists Mill and Cairnes being taken as typical -- whose names have been associated with deductive methods in modern science. With a fine sense of truth they saw that the notion of causal continuity, as a premise of scientific generalisation, is an essentially metaphysical postulate; and they avoided its treacherous ground by denying it, and construing causal sequence to mean a uniformity of co-existences and successions simply. But, since a strict uniformity is nowhere to be observed at first hand in the phenomena with which the investigator is occupied, it has to be found by a laborious interpretation of the phenomena and a diligent abstraction and allowance for disturbing circumstances, whatever may be the meaning of a disturbing circumstance where causal continuity is denied. In this work of interpretation and expurgation the investigator proceeds on a conviction of the orderliness of the natural sequence. "Natura non facit saltum": a maxim which has no meaning within the stricter limits of the associational theory of knowledge.

Before anything can be said as to the orderliness of the sequence, a point of view must be chosen by the speculator, with respect to which the sequence in question does or does not fulfill this condition of orderliness; that is to say, with respect to which it is a sequence. The endeavor to avoid all metaphysical premises fails here as everywhere. The associationists, to whom economics owes its transition from the older classical phase to the modern or quasi-classical, chose as their guiding point of view the metaphysical postulate of congruity, -- in substance, the "similarity" of the associationist theory of knowledge. This must be called their proton pseudos, if associationism pure and simple is to be accepted. The notion of congruity works out in laws of resemblance and equivalence, in both of which it is plain to the modern psychologist that a metaphysical ground of truth, antecedent to and controlling empirical data, is assumed. But the use of the postulate of congruence as a test of scientific truth has the merit of avoiding all open dealing with an imputed substantiality of the data handled, such as would be involved in the overt use of the concept of causation. The data are congruous among themselves, as items of knowledge; and they may therefore be handled in a logical synthesis and concatenation on the basis of this congruence alone, without committing the scientist to an imputation of a kinetic or motor relation between them. The metaphysics of process is thereby avoided, in appearance. The sequences are uniform or consistent with one another, taken as articles of theoretical synthesis simply" and so they become elements of a system or discipline of knowledge in which the test of theoretical truth is the congruence of the system with its premises.

In all this there is a high-wrought appearance of matter-of-fact, and all metaphysical subreption of a non-empirical or non-mechanical standard of reality or substantiality is avoided in appearance. The generalisations which make up such a system of knowledge are, in this way, stated in terms of the system itself; and when a competent formulation of the alleged uniformities has been so made in terms of their congruity or equivalence with the prime postulates of the system, the work of theoretical inquiry is done.

The concrete premises from which proceeds the systematic knowledge of this generation of economists are certain very concise assumptions concerning human nature, and certain slightly less concise generalisations of physical fact,(5*) presumed to be mechanically empirical generalisations. These postulates afford the standard of normality. Whatever situation or course of events can be shown to express these postulates without mitigation is normal; and wherever a departuRe from this normal course of things occurs, it is due to disturbing causes,that is to say, to causes not comprised in the main premises of the science, -- and such departures are to be taken account of by way of qualification. Such departures and such qualification are constantly present in the facts to be handled by the science; but, being not congruous with the underlying postulates, they have no place in the body of the science. The laws of the science, that which makes up the economist's theoretical knowledge, are laws of the normal case. The normal case does not occur in concrete fact. These laws are, therefore, in Cairnes's terminology, "hypothetical" truths; and the science is a "hypothetical" science. They apply to concrete facts only as the facts are interpreted and abstracted from, in the light of the underlying postulates. The science is, therefore, a theory of the normal case, a discussion of the concrete facts of life in respect of their degree of approximation to the normal case. That is to say, it is a taxonomic science.

Of course, in the work actually done by these economists this standpoint of rigorous normality is not consistently maintained; nor is the unsophisticated imputation of causality to the facts under discussion consistently avoided. The associationist postulate, that causal sequence means empirical uniformity simply, is in great measure forgotten when the subject-matter of the science is handled in detail. Especially is it true that in Mill the dry light of normality is greatly relieved by a strong common sense. But the great truths or laws of the science remain hypothetical laws; and the test of scientific reality is congruence with the hypothetical laws, not coincidence with matter-of-fact events.

The earlier, more archaic metaphysics of the science, which saw in the orderly correlation and sequence of events a constraining guidance of an extra-causal, teleological kind, in this way becomes a metaphysics of normality which asserts no extra-causal constraint over events, but contents itself with establishing correlations, equivalencies, homologies, and theories concerning the conditions of an economic equilibrium. The movement, the process of economic life, is not overlooked, and it may even be said that it is not neglected, but the pure theory, in its final deliverances, deals not with the dynamics, but with the statics of the case. The concrete subject-matter of the science is, of course, the process of economic life, -- that is unavoidably the case, -- and in so far the discussion must be accepted as work bearing on the dynamics of the phenomena discussed; but even then it remains true that the aim of this work in dynamics is a determination and taxis of the outcome of the process under discussion rather than a theory of the process as such. The process is rated in terms of the equilibrium to which it tends or should tend, not conversely. The outcome of the process, taken in its relation of equivalence within the system, is the point at which the inquiry comes to rest. It is not primarily the point of departure for an inquiry into what may follow. The science treats of a balanced system rather than of a proliferation. In this lies its characteristic difference from the later evolutionary sciences. It is this characteristic bent of the science that leads its spokesman, Cairnes, to turn so kindly to chemistry rather than to the organic sciences, when he seeks an analogy to economics among the physical sciences.(6*) What Cairnes has in mind in his appeal to chemistry is, of course, the received, extremely taxonomic (systematic) chemistry of his own time, not the tentatively genetic theories of a slightly later day. It may seem that in the characterisation just offered of the standpoint of normality in economics there is too strong an implication of colorlessness and impartiality. The objection holds as regards much of the work of the modern economists of the classical line. It will hold true even as to much of Cairnes's work, but it cannot be admitted as regards Cairnes's ideal of scientific aim and methods. The economists whose theories Cairnes received and developed, assuredly did not pursue the discussion of the normal case with an utterly dispassionate animus. They had still enough of the older teleological metaphysics left to give color to the accusation brought against them that they were advocates of laissez-faire. The preconception of the utilitarians, -- in substance the natural-rights preconception, -- that unrestrained human conduct will result in the greatest human happiness, retains so much of its force in Cairnes's time as is implied in the then current assumption that what is normal is also right. The economists, and Cairnes among them, not only are concerned to find out what is normal and to determine what consummation answers to the normal, but they also are at pains to approve that consummation. It is this somewhat uncritical and often unavowed identification of the normal with the right that gives colorable ground for the widespread vulgar prejudice, to which Cairnes draws attention,(7*) that political economy "sanctions" one social arrangement and "condemns" another. And it is against this uncritical identification of two essentially unrelated principles or categories that Cairnes's essay on "Political Economy and Laissez-faire," and in good part also that on Bastiat, are directed. But, while this is one of the many points at which Cairnes has substantially advanced the ideals of the science, his own concluding argument shows him to have been but half-way emancipated from the prejudice, even while most effectively combating it.(8*) It is needless to point out that the like prejudice is still present in good vigor in many later economists who have had the full benefit of Cairnes's teachings on this head.(9*) Considerable as

Cairnes's achievement in this matter undoubtedly was, it effected a mitigation rather than an elimination of the untenable metaphysics against which he contended.

The advance in the general point of view from animistic teleology to taxonomy is shown in a curiously succinct manner in a parenthetical clause of Cairnes's in the chapter on Normal Value.(10*) With his acceptance of the later point of view involved in the use of the new term, Cairnes becomes the interpreter of the received theoretical results. The received positions are not subjected to a destructive criticism. The aim is to complete them where they fall short and to cut off what may be needless or what may run beyond the safe ground of scientific generalisation. In his work of redaction, Cairnes does not avow -- probably he is not sensible of -- any substantial shifting of the point of view or any change in the accepted ground of theoretic reality. But his advance to an unteleological taxonomy none the less changes the scope and aim of his theoretical discussion. The discussion of Normal Value may be taken in illustration.

Cairnes is not content to find (with Adam Smith) that value will "naturally" coincide with or be measured by cost of production, or even (with Mill) that cost of production must, in the long run, "necessarily" determine value. "This is to take a much too limited view of the range of this phenomenon." (11*) He is concerned to determine not only this general tendency of values to a normal, but all those characteristic circumstances as well which condition this tendency and which determine the normal to which values tend. His inquiry pursues the phenomena of value in a normal economic system rather than the manner and rate of approach of value relations to a teleologically or hedonistically defensible consummation. It therefore becomes an exhaustive but very discriminating analysis of the circumstances that bear upon market values, with a view to determine what circumstances are normally present; that is to say, what circumstances conditioning value are commonly effective and at the same time in consonance with the premises of economic theory, These effective conditions, in so far as they are not counted anomalous and, therefore, to be set aside in the theoretical discussion, are the circumstances under which a hedonistic valuation process in any modern industrial community is held perforce to take place, -- the circumstances which are held to enforce a recognition and rating of the pleasure-bearing capacity of facts. They are not, as under the earlier cost-of-production doctrines, the circumstances which determine the magnitude of the forces spent in the production of the valuable article. Therefore, the normal (natural) value is no longer (as with Adam Smith, and even to some extent with his classical successors) the primary or initial fact in value theory, the substantial fact of which the market value is an approximate expression and by which the latter is controlled. The argument does not, as formerly, set out from that expenditure of personal force which was once conceived to constitute the substantial value of goods, and then construe market value to be an approximate and uncertain expression of this substantial fact. The direction in which the argument runs is rather the reverse of this. The point of departure is taken from the range of market values and the process of bargaining by which these values are determined. This latter is taken to be a process of discrimination between various kinds and degrees of discomfort, and the average or consistent outcome of such a process of bargaining constitutes normal value. It is only by virtue of a presumed equivalence between the discomfort undergone and the concomitant expenditure, whether of labor or of wealth, that the normal value so determined is conceived to be an expression of the productive force that goes into the creation of the valuable goods. Cost being only in uncertain equivalence with sacrifice or discomfort, as between different persons, the factor of cost falls into the background; and the process of bargaining, which is in the foreground, being a process of valuation, a balancing of individual demand and supply, it follows that a law of reciprocal demand comes in to supplant the law of cost. In all this the proximate causes at work in the determination of values are plainly taken account of more adequately than in earlier cost-of-production doctrines; but they are taken account of with a view to explaining the mutual adjustment and interrelation of elements in a system rather than to explain either a developmental sequence or the working out of a fore-ordained end.

This revision of the cost-of-production doctrine, whereby it takes the form of a law of reciprocal demand, is in good part effected by a consistent reduction of cost to terms of sacrifice, -- a reduction more consistently carried through by Cairnes than it had been by earlier hedonists, and extended by Cairnes's successors with even more far-reaching results. By this step the doctrine of cost is not only brought into closer accord with the neo-hedonistic premises, in that it in a greater degree throws the stress upon the factor of personal discrimination, but it also gives the doctrine a more general bearing upon economic conduct and increases its serviceability as a comprehensive principle for the classification of economic phenomena. In the further elaboration of the hedonistic theory of value at the hands of Jevons and the Austrians the same principle of sacrifice comes to serve as the chief ground of procedure.

Of the foundations of later theory, in so far as the postulates of later economists differ characteristically from those of Mill and Cairnes, little can be said in this place. Nothing but the very general features of the later development can be taken up; and even these general features of the existing theoretic situation can not be handled with the same confidence as the corresponding features of a past phase of speculation. With respect to writers of the present or the more recent past the work of natural selection, as between variants of scientific aim and animus and between more or less divergent points of view, has not yet taken effect; and it would be over-hazardous to attempt an anticipation of the results of the selection that lies in great part yet in the future. As regards the directions of theoretical work suggested by the names of Professor Marshall, Mr. Cannan, Professor Clark, Mr. Pierson, Austrian Professor Loria, Professor Schmoller, the group, -- no off-hand decision is admissible as between these candidates for the honor, or, better, for the work, of continuing the main current of economic speculation and inquiry. No attempt will here be made even to pass a verdict on the relative claims of the recognised two or three main "schools" of theory, beyond the somewhat obvious finding that, for the purpose in hand, the so-called Austrian school is scarcely distinguishable from the neo-classical, unless it be in the different distribution of emphasis. The divergence between the modernised classical views, on the one hand, and the historical and Marxist schools, on the other hand, is wider, -- so much so, indeed, as to bar out a consideration of the postulates of the latter under the same head of inquiry with the former. The inquiry, therefore, confines itself to the one line standing most obviously in unbroken continuity with that body of classical economics whose life history has been traced in outline above. And, even for this phase of modernised classical economics, it seems necessary to limit discussion, for the present, to a single strain, selected as standing peculiarly close to the classical source, at the same time that it shows unmistakable adaptation to the later habits of thought and methods of knowledge.

For this later development in the classical line of political economy, Mr. Keynes's book may fairly be taken as the maturest exposition of the aims and ideals of the science; while Professor Marshall excellently exemplifies the best work that is being done under the guidance of the classical antecedents. As, after a lapse of a dozen or fifteen years from Cairnes's days of full conviction, Mr. Keynes interprets the aims of modern economic science, it has less of the "hypothetical" character assigned it by Cairnes. that is to say, it confines its inquiry less closely to the ascertainment of the normal case and the interpretative subsumption of facts under the normal. It takes fuller account of the genesis and developmental continuity of all features of modern economic life, gives more and closer attention to institutions and their history. This is, no doubt, due, in part at least, to impulse received from German economists; and in so far it also reflects the peculiarly vague and bewildered attitude of protest that characterises the earlier expositions of the historical school. To the same essentially extraneous source is traceable the theoretic blur embodied in Mr. Keynes's attitude of tolerance towards the conception of economics as a "normative" science having to do with "economic ideals", or an "applied economics" having to do with "economic precepts." (12*) An inchoate departure from the consistent taxonomic ideals shows itself in the tentative resort to historical and genetic formulations, as well as in Mr. Keynes's pervading inclination to define the scope of the science, not by exclusion of what are conceived to be non-economic phenomena, but by disclosing a point of view from which all phenomena are seen to be economic facts. The science comes to be characterised not by the delimitation of a range of facts, as in Cairnes, (13*) but as an inquiry into the bearing which all facts have upon men's economic activity. It is no longer that certain phenomena belong within the science, but rather that the science is concerned with any and all phenomena as seen from the point of view of the economic interest. Mr. Keynes does not go fully to the length which this last proposition indicates. He finds (14*) that political economy" treats of the phenomena arising out of the economic activities of mankind in society"; but, while the discussion by which he leads up to this definition might be construed to say that all the activities of mankind in society have an economic bearing, and should therefore come within the view of the science, Mr. Keynes does not carry out his elucidation of the matter to that broad conclusion. Neither can it be said that modern political economy has, in practice, taken on the scope and character which this extreme position would assign it.

The passage from which the above citation is taken is highly significant also in another and related bearing, and it is at the same time highly characteristic of the most effective modernised classical economics. The subject matter of the science has come to be the "economic activities" of mankind, and the phenomena in which these activities manifest themselves. So Professor Marshall's work, for instance, is, in aim, even if not always in achievement, a theoretical handling of human activity in its economic bearing, -- an inquiry into the multiform phases and ramifications of that process of valuation of the material means of life by virtue of which man is an economic agent. And still it remains an inquiry directed to the determination of the conditions of an equilibrium of activities and a quiescent normal situation. It is not in any eminent degree an inquiry into cultural or institutional development as affected by economic exigencies or by the economic interest of the men whose activities are analysed and portrayed. Any sympathetic reader of Professor Marshall's great work -- and that must mean every reader -- comes away with a sense of swift and smooth movement and interaction of parts; but it is the movement of a consummately conceived and self-balanced mechanism, not that of a cumulatively unfolding process or an institutional adaptation to cumulatively unfolding exigencies. The taxonomic bearing is, after all, the dominant feature. It is significant of the same point that even in his discussion of such vitally dynamic features of the economic process as the differential effectiveness of different laborers or of different industrial plants, as well as of the differential advantages of consumers, Professor Marshall resorts to an adaptation of so essentially taxonomic a category as the received concept of rent. Rent is a pecuniary category, a category of income, which is essentially a final term, not a category of the motor term, work or interest.(15*) It is not a factor or a feature of the process of industrial life, but a phenomenon of the pecuniary situation which emerges from this process under given conventional circumstances. However far-reaching and various the employment of the rent concept in economic theory has been, it has through all permutations remained, what it was to begin with, a rubric in the classification of incomes. It is a pecuniary, not an industrial category. In so far as resort is had to the rent concept in the formulation of a theory of the industrial process, -- as in Professor Marshall's work, -- it comes to a statement of the process in terms of its residue. Let it not seem presumptuous to say that. great and permanent as is the value of Professor Marshall's exposition of quasi-rents and the like, the endeavor which it involves to present in terms of a concluded system what is of the nature of a fluent process has made the exposition unduly bulky, unwieldy, and inconsequent.

There is a curious reminiscence of the perfect taxonomic

day in Mr. Keynes's characterisation of political economy as a "positive science," "the sole province of which is to establish economic uniformities"; (16*) and, in this resort to the associationist expedient of defining a natural law as a" uniformity," Mr. Keynes is also borne out by Professor Marshall.(17*) But this and other survivals of the taxonomic terminology, or even of the taxonomic canons of procedure, do not binder the economists of the modern school from doing effective work of a character that must be rated as genetic rather than taxonomic. Professor Marshall's work in economics is not unlike that of Asa Gray in botany, who, while working in great part within the lines of "systematic botany" and adhering to its terminology, and on the whole also to its point of view, very materially furthered the advance of the science outside the scope of taxonomy.

Professor Marshall shows an aspiration to treat economic life as a development; and, at least superficially, much of his work bears the appearance of being a discussion of this kind. In this endeavor his work is typical of what is aimed at by many of the later economists. The aim shows itself with a persistent recurrence in his Principles. His chosen maxim is, "Natura non facit saltum," -- a maxim that might well serve to designate the prevailing attitude of modern economists towards questions of economic development as well as towards questions of classification or of economic policy. His insistence on the continuity of development and of the economic structure of communities is a characteristic of the best work along the later line of classical political economy. All this gives an air of evolutionism to the work. Indeed, the work of the neo-classical economics might be compared, probably without offending any of its adepts, with that of the early generation of Darwinians, though such a comparison might somewhat shrewdly have to avoid any but superficial features. Economists of the present day are commonly evolutionists, in a general way. They commonly accept, as other men do, the general results of the evolutionary speculation in those directions in which the evolutionary method has made its way. But the habit of handling by evolutionist methods the facts with which their own science is concerned has made its way among the economists to but a very uncertain degree.

The prime postulate of evolutionary science, the preconception constantly underlying the inquiry, is the notion of a cumulative causal sequence; and writers on economics are in the habit of recognising that the phenomena with which they are occupied are subject to such a law of development. Expressions of assent to this proposition abound. But the economists have not worked out or hit upon a method by which the inquiry in economics may consistently be conducted under the guidance of this postulate. Taking Professor Marshall as exponent, it appears that, while the formulations of economic theory are not conceived to be arrived at by way of an inquiry into the developmental variation of economic institutions and the like, the theorems arrived at are held, and no doubt legitimately, to apply to the past,(18*) and with due reserve also to the future, phases of the development. But these theorems apply to the various phases of the development not as accounting for the developmental sequence, but as limiting the range of variation. They say little, if anything, as to the order of succession, as to the derivation and the outcome of any given phase, or as to the causal relation of one phase of any given economic convention or scheme of relations to any other. They indicate the conditions of survival to which any innovation is subject, supposing the innovation to have taken place, not the conditions of variational growth. The economic laws, the" statements of uniformity," are therefore, when construed in an evolutionary bearing, theorems concerning the superior or the inferior limit of persistent innovations, as the case may be.(19*) It is only in this negative, selective bearing that the current economic laws are held to be laws of developmental continuity; and it should be added that they have hitherto found but relatively scant application at the hands of the economists, even for this purpose.

Again, as applied to economic activities under a given situation, as laws governing activities in equilibrium, the economic laws are, in the main, laws of the limits within which economic action of a given purpose runs. They are theorems as to the limits which the economic (commonly the pecuniary) interest imposes upon the range of activities to which the other life interests of men incite, rather than theorems as to the manner and degree in which the economic interest creatively shapes the general scheme of life. In great part they formulate the normal inhibitory effect of economic exigencies rather than the cumulative modification and diversification of human activities through the economic interest, by initiating and guiding habits of life and of thought. This, of course, does not go to say that economists are at all slow to credit the economic exigencies with a large share in the growth of culture; but, while claims of this kind are large and recurrent, it remains true that the laws which make up the framework of economic doctrine are, when construed as generalisations of causal relation, laws of conservation and selection, not of genesis and proliferation. The truth of this, which is but a commonplace generalisation, might be shown in detail with respect to such fundamental theorems as the laws of rent, of profits, of wages, of the increasing or diminishing returns of industry, of population, of competitive prices, of cost of production.

In consonance with this quasi-evolutionary tone of the neo-classical political economy, or as an expression of it, comes the further clarified sense that nowadays attaches to the terms "normal" and economic "laws." The laws have gained in colorlessness, until it can no longer be said that the concept of normality implies approval of the phenomena to which it is applied.(20*) They are in an increasing degree laws of conduct, though they still continue to formulate conduct in hedonistic terms; that is to say, conduct is construed in terms of its sensuous effect, not in terms of its teleological content. The light of the science is a drier light than it was, but it continues to be shed upon the accessories of human action rather than upon the process itself. The categories employed for the purpose of knowing this economic conduct with which the scientists occupy themselves are not the categories under which the men at whose hands the action takes place themselves apprehend their own action at the instant of acting. Therefore, economic conduct still continues to be somewhat mysterious to the economists; and they are forced to content themselves with adumbrations whenever the discussion touches this central, substantial fact.

All this, of course, is intended to convey no dispraise of the work done, nor in any way to disparage the theories which the passing generation of economists have elaborated, or the really great and admirable body of Knowledge which they have brought under the hand of the science; but only to indicate the direction in which the inquiry in its later phases -- not always with full consciousness -- is shifting as regards its categories and its point of view. The discipline of life in a modern community, particularly the industrial life, strongly reinforced by the modern sciences, has divested our knowledge of non-human phenomena of that fullness of self-directing life that was once imputed to them, and has reduced this knowledge to terms of opaque causal sequence. It has thereby narrowed the range of discretionary, teleological action to the human agent alone; and so it is compelling our knowledge of human conduct, in so far as it is distinguished from the non-human, to fall into teleological terms. Foot-pounds, calories, geometrically progressive procreation, and doses of capital, have not been supplanted by the equally uncouth denominations of habits, propensities, aptitudes, and conventions, nor does there seem to be any probability that they will be; but the discussion which continues to run in terms of the former class of concepts is in an increasing degree seeking support in concepts of the latter class.

NOTES:

1. So, e.g., Roscher, Comte, the early socialists, J.S. Mill, and

later Spencer, Schaeffle, Wagner.

2. "Let us not confound the statement that human interests are at one with the statement that class interests

are at one. The latter I believe to be as false as the former is true... But accepting the major premises of the syllogism, that the interests of human beings are fundamentally the same, how as to the minor? -- how as to the assumption that people know their interests in the sense in which they are identical with the interests of

others, and that they spontaneously follow them in this sense?" -- Cairnes, Essays in Political Economy (London, 1873), p. 245. This question cannot consistently be asked by an adherent of the stricter hedonism.

3. Bastiat, quoted by Cairnes, Essays, p. 319.

4. It may be remarked, by the way, that the use of the differential calculus and similar mathematical expedients in the discussion of marginal utility and the like, proceeds on the psychological ground, and that the theoretical results so arrived at are valid to the full extent only if this hedonistic psychology is accepted.

5. See, e.g., Cairnes, Character and Logical Method (New York), p. 71.

6. Character and Logical Method, p. 62.

7. Essays in Political Economy, pp. 260-264.

8. See especially Essays, pp. 263, 264.

9. It may be interesting to point out that the like identification of the categories of normality and right gives the dominant note of Mr. Spencer's ethical and social philosophy, and that later economists of the classical and social philosophy to

be Spencerians.

10. "Normal value (called by Adam Smith and Ricardo "natural value," and by Mill "necessary value," but best expressed, it seems to me, by the term which I have used)." Leading Principles (New York), p. 45.

11. Leading Principles, p. 45.

12. Scope and Method of Political Economy (London, 1891), chaps. i and ii.

13. Character and Logical Method; e.g., Lecture II, especially pp. 53, 54, 71.

14. Scope and Method of Political Economy, chap. iii,

particularly p. 97.

15. "Interest" is, of course, here used in the sense which it has in modern psychological discussion.

16. Scope and Method of Political Economy, p. 46.

17. Principles of Economics, Vol. 1, Book 1, chap. vi, sect. 6, especially p. 105 (3rd edition).

18. See, e.g., Professor Marshall's "Reply" to Professor Cunningham in the Economic Journal for 1892, pp. 508-113.

19. This is well illustrated by what Professor Marshall says of the Ricardian law of rent in his "Reply" cited above.

20. See, e.g., Marshall, Principles, Book I, chap. vi, sect. 6, pp. 105-108. The like dispassionateness is visible in most other modern writers on theory; as, e.g., Clark, Cannan, and the Austrians.

Printed in Great Britain
by Amazon